CALEDONIA
Along the Grand River

The scenic park at the Caledonia dam is lined with fishermen during the spring season. The summer months bring tourists and residents to this popular site along the Grand River.

CALEDONIA

Along the Grand River

BARBARA MARTINDALE

NATURAL HERITAGE / NATURAL HISTORY INC.

Caledonia: Along the Grand River
by Barbara Martindale

Published by Natural Heritage / Natural History Inc.
P.O. Box 95, Station "O", Toronto, Ontario M4A 2M8

Design and typesetting: Robin Brass Studio
Printed and bound in Canada by Hignell Printing Limited,
Winnipeg, Manitoba

Canadian Cataloguing in Publication Data

Martindale, Barbara
Caledonia : along the Grand River

ISBN 0-920474-81-0

1. Caledonia (Haldimand, Ont.) – History.
I. Title

FC3099.C34M37 1994   971.3'36   C94-93-437-9
F1059.5.C34M37 1994

FRONT COVER: Bowling Green at Edinburgh Square Heritage
and Cultural Centre. (Courtesy Jean McClung)
BACK COVER: Raft Race on the Grand River. (Courtesy Jean McClung)

Natural Heritage / Natural History Inc. gratefully acknowledges the assistance
of the Canada Council, the Ontario Arts Council, and the Government of
Ontario through the Ministry of Citizenship, Tourism and Recreation.

To the historians of Caledonia ~
Mary Nelles
Earl Gillespie
Harrison Martindale

A 1940 street scene looking north from the bridge.

Contents

Prologue 9

Introduction 13

When It All Began 15

From the Haldimand Grant to the Grand River
Navigation Company 15

There's More to the Legend: Captain John Norton 17

By River and Rail 23

Navigation on the Grand River 23

Transportation on the Rails 26

Caledonia Fair 32

The Incurable Optimist 35

The McKinnon Lifestyle 37

James Little 39

William Moore 42

Well Loved and Remembered 43

The Good Old Days of the Opera House 43

A "Lovable" Constable 45

The MacGregor Concert Bureau 46

O.T. Scott 49

A Real Sweetheart: Eva Marlene Heddle 51

The Rt. Honourable Arthur Meighen (1874–1960) 52

Pauline Johnson: Famous Canadian Poet 53

Peter Robertson, Inventor of the Robertson Screwnail 57

An Area Knight: Sir Byron Edmund Walker 58

William Doyle 60

Bruce E. French 60

Mrs. Fleming's "English Pink Ointment" 61

He Walked Alone 63

The Six Nations Artist 64

LANDMARKS 67

Edinburgh Square 67

The Old Town Hall 69

The Landmark – The Caledonia Bridge 73

Former Bridges 75

The Bridge Without A Reason 77

The Old Mill 78

Built To Take Tolls 79

THE OLDEST SURVIVING BUSINESS: CALEDONIA'S
NEWSPAPER 81

FOUNDRIES AND FACTORIES 84

Caledonia's Gypsum History 85

THERE WAS ONCE A CONCERT BAND 89

LETTERS FROM WORLD WAR I 91

MORE STORIES OF TOWN LIFE 95

The Bakery – Caledonia's Oldest Family Business 95

Caledonia's Women's Institute 97

A Husband's View of the Women's Institute 98

Dentistry of Another Era 99

Thousands Are Called Home in 1927 99

An Anniversary Broadcast 101

Hockey Popularity 103

Baseball 105

The Day The Ice Goes Out 106

BIG CREEK BOAT FARM 108

CALEDONIA SCENES 110

MEMORIES 112

by O.T. Scott, 1956

NOTES AND PICTURE CREDITS 115

ACKNOWLEDGMENTS & INFORMATION 119

SOURCES 120

INDEX 121

Prologue

Caledonia's settlement isn't too different from other small towns along the Grand River, now designated as a Canadian Heritage River. The area along the Grand River banks was ripe for settlement during the early 1800's, when river transportation played a major role in the pioneering of this country. Ultimately canal building in the 1830's had an effect on where settlements would spring up. Caledonia's development is a result.

Of course, there is much more to the story when we learn of two early villages, one to the east and the other to the west. Who were the movers and shakers to pull those two villages into what would be Caledonia?

In this era, some 150 years later, Caledonia and area people are becoming increasingly proud of their heritage. The history of landmarks, buildings, businesses and forefathers is important to them. Whether they are new to the community, longtime residents or visitors who are interested in features, symbols, ancestors or progress, the meaning behind what once was is significant. It gives us all a certain perspective.

For this reason, *Caledonia: Along the Grand River* has been written. There are at least another ten volumes to the Caledonia and area story, but one has to begin and end somewhere in one publication.

The simple, story-like style was intentional. For most people it will provide enough information to know a bit about the area's history in which they either live or have an interest. For the historian who wants more detail, it will whet their appetite to search further.

There are many, many people who have provided information for this book. Each and everyone will know who they are, and the contribution they made whether it was filling in a detail, lending a valued photograph or presenting information about a family member never told nor published before. Thank you.

Caledonia, as a community, is fortunate to have continuous publication of its newspaper, *The Grand River Sachem*, since 1856. Today, anyone wanting to do research can do so through its pages on microfilm in a public location at Edinburgh Square Heritage and Cultural Centre. The *Sachem* and Edinburgh Square's Centre also were invaluable resources for this book.

It was Barry Penhale of Natural Heritage / Natural History Inc., who encouraged the writing of *Caledonia: Along the Grand River*. His foresight, editorial skills and desire to publish such a book made it possible.

BARBARA A. MARTINDALE

Village of Caledonia,
County of Haldimand
survey map, c. 1877.
(Historical Atlas of Haldimand and Norfolk Counties)

Caledonia Fairgrounds as it was for the Fair in 1913.

Introduction

If there is a certain spirit about a town, it comes from the people who live there. It comes from being a proud Canadian, proud of a heritage within Canada and its province. The roots established in a hometown environment last forever. The courage of our forefathers who began with little more than strong backs and tough hands in a new land is astounding but admirable. The flourishing villages and farms along with mills passed on to the following generations provided the foundation for the country.

More than 150 years ago, Ranald McKinnon of Scottish ancestry, made sure the community of Caledonia took on his heritage when he named the town, its streets and squares. Edinburgh, the only town square left today, retains the town hall built in McKinnon's time. Now a Heritage and Cultural Centre, it preserves the history and artifacts of our past and passes on the legacy left by McKinnon and others of his era.

The town is growing very rapidly these days with new developments branching out into what were once rural areas. Less than twenty years ago the population was stagnant at 3000. Now the statistics boast almost double that. Caledonia was once a town within the County of Haldimand, surrounded by the townships of Oneida and Seneca, with the Six Nations Reserve found at their borders. Today these areas and Caledonia, along with Cayuga, Hagersville and their surrounding districts, are contained within the Town of Haldimand, one of six area municipalities within the Regional Municipality of Haldimand Norfolk.

Ours is a picturesque, nostalgic community where one can walk the banks of the Grand River along a path that was once a towpath. This towpath is the tangible reminder of the heyday of river navigation, the reason for the town's settlement in the 1830's. The historic nine span bridge in the heart of town, the only one of its type in Canada, is of significant interest and another link with the river. With the recent designation of the Grand River as a Canadian Heritage River a new era and relationship begins.

Renowned for its natural beauty and cultural diversity, Caledonia, situated only a few miles south of Hamilton and within an hour's drive of major cities in southern Ontario, has location as a key reason for its rapid growth. Other contributing factors can be found in the small town atmosphere, the nature of the people and their pride in their heritage.

We owe much to those who have gone before for they are the true links to our present and future. One such person was O.T. Scott who described what Caledonia was, and still is, in a poem written in 1927:

Our Village does not claim to be
The largest in the land.
We're just a pretty little burg
Along the River Grand.
But we have points of interest
That make life here worthwhile
And bring you home contented
When you've travelled many a mile.

And we in business want to build,
And keep our Town's good name,
To pull together, lend a hand
And learn to play the game.
And so a toast, I give to you,
I ask you drink it deep -
The Town of Caledonia
My town – to build and keep.

THE HALDIMAND GRANT
1784

Following the American Revolution Sir Frederick Haldimand Governor-in-Chief of Canada, granted to the Six Nations of the Iroquois a tract of land extending for six miles on both sides of the Grand River from its source to Lake Erie. This grant was made in recognition of their services as allies of the British Crown during the war, and to recompense them for the loss of their former lands in northern New York State. In later years large areas of this tract including portions of the present counties of Haldimand, Brant, Waterloo and Wellington, were sold to white settlers.

Erected by the Ontario Archaeological and Historic Sites Board

Plaque commemorating the Haldimand Grant of 1784.

When It All Began

From the Haldimand Grant to the Grand River Navigation Company
Caledonia's story begins with the aftermath of the American Revolution. On October 25, 1784, the British Crown gave Mohawk Chief Joseph Brant and his Six Nations Confederacy six miles of land on either side of the Grand River beginning from its mouth at Lake Erie to its source in present-day Dufferin County. This land grant was given in gratitude for their services and loyalty to the Crown during the American revolutionary war and in response to their application for recompense for their lands lost to the United States.

The grant was completed by Sir Frederick Haldimand, Governor-in-Chief of Canada, after whom the county is named and subsequently the entire regional municipality. That same year Chief Brant invited some white Loyalist friends who were refugees from the Revolution, to settle with him in the Grand River Valley. In turn Brant gave them tracts of land along the river.

Portrait of Joseph Brant (Thayendanegea), the Mohawk leader.

One of these friends was Henry Nelles and his sons. They were allotted a block in Seneca Township, three miles back from the river bank and three miles broad, plus a small tract in Oneida on the south side. Adam Young and his sons were also given a large tract in Seneca further east beyond York, a village along the banks of the Grand. There were no roads or easy access and no improvements in the area. The Nelles and Young families began the back breaking labour of clearing the land by hand. Later others would come and settle mainly around Oneida.

Shortly after 1830 the government, with the consent of the Chiefs, decided to sell all the remaining portions of the reserve in Haldimand, except for a small section in Oneida, and open this area for development. The proceeds were to be invested for the benefit of the Indians, with the interest on the investment being paid in goods

Sir Frederick Haldimand.

such as guns, blankets, and ammunition. Consequently, a treaty was concluded that resulted in the surrender of the lands to the government and the opening up of the townships for white settlement.

In 1832 a bill was passed by the provincial government authorizing canal and lock building on the Grand, or Ouse River as it had been known. The success of the Rideau Canal and the new Welland Canal's feeder line to Dunnville had opened up the Grand, making commercial navigation possible. Already the Dunnville Dam, which had been built in 1829, allowed boats to travel through Cayuga to the nearby village of Indiana.

In the entrepreneurial spirit of the time The Grand River Navigation Company was formed. With John Jackson as engineer, more dams, canals and locks were to be built. Travel on up the river from Indiana to Brantford could be made possible. Timber, gypsum and grain products would move more rapidly. By 1833 dams one, two and three were completed at Indiana, York and Sims Locks. Dam four, just east of what we know as Caledonia today, was in place in 1834.

The Navigation Company laid out small villages on north and south banks of the Grand. The village of Seneca was located on the north bank at Dam four, while the village of South Seneca was on the south bank. By 1834 Jacob Turner, the contractor for dam four, was operating a sawmill at Seneca Village. Settlers were beginning to establish other businesses in both the north and south sites. Dam five, about a mile to the west at Oneida, was yet to be built. Once Ranald McKinnon was assigned as the contractor, he built a sawmill on the north bank right at that location as was the practise of the time. This marked the beginning of the village of Oneida on the north bank and Sunnyside on the south bank.

When McKinnon first arrived in the area he came upon Bryant's Corners, a hamlet consisting of two log houses and a tavern owned by Mr. Bryant. Today, Bryant's Corners is the main corner of Caledonia at Caithness and Argyle Street, midway between what was then Seneca Village and Oneida Village.

There's More To The Legend: Captain John Norton

He deserved more acclaim than he was given. He did not deserve the legendary inaccuracy he received. A story of John Norton, passed down through the years and written under the title of *The Last Duel in Canada* created some widespread notoriety, but there was much more to John Norton than the duel fought in the latter stages of his life.

Captain John Norton (Teyoninhokarawen) was born about 1760 to a Cherokee father and a Scottish mother in the country of the Cherokees. In 1795 he arrived at the Grand River settlements to be an interpreter among the Grand River Indians. His years of education in Scotland, his linguistic abilities and personal flair had prepared him for leadership with his people.

In 1823 when John Norton was about 60 years old, he owned Hillhouse, a mansion of the day located atop a hill along the Grand River just east of what is now known as Caledonia. By then he was a prominent citizen accepted as a Mohawk of the Grand River community and highly respected among those he lobbied in England on behalf of the Indian

This portrait of Major John Norton, by Thomas Phillips, R.D., Syon House, Brentford, was originally published in *The Journal of Major John Norton 1816*, Toronto, The Champlain Society, 1970.

nations. But he left after the duel fought at Hillhouse, never to be heard of again.

It wasn't until 1970 when the Champlain Society of Canada published *The Journal of John Norton 1916*, edited with introductions and notes by Carl F. Klink and James J. Talman, that the full Norton story became known.[1] The Champlain Society was given permission to print the manuscript by His Grace, the tenth Duke of Northumberland.

Captain Norton had been commissioned by the second Duke of Northumberland to write this journal while documenting a journey of a thousand miles down the Ohio in 1809. In this account he described the Five Nations as well as describing his way to the Cherokee country of Tennessee in 1809-10 and recorded his campaigns in the War of 1812-14. Norton's journals are published in two volumes with forty pages given to a table of contents and a dedication to the second duke, nine hundred and sixty-seven pages for text and twenty-three pages of vocabulary.

By 1799 Joseph Brant had conferred the title of war chief upon him. It is said that his accomplishments exceeded Brant's anticipations as Norton lobbied on behalf of the Indians, taught them agriculture and dealt with their land claims. Following Joseph Brant's death on November 24, 1807, John Norton became their respected spokesman and leader.

Norton's exceptional career encompassed the difficult early history of Upper Canada. Especially complicated were dealings concerning the place of the Six Nations, their land claims and the lobbying that had to be conducted with the British Government during Joseph Brant's time and after.

One description of Norton tells us that he spoke the language of about twelve different Indian nations, as well as English, French, German and Spanish, and that he was an avid reader in possession of all the modern literature of the day. Another said he was a man of great natural acuteness, possessing much reflective ability united with a sense of religion and an ardent devotion to the interest of his tribes. A physical description tells us that "he was 6 feet tall, well made, active, possessing a dark complexion, mild with pleasing manners and prone to wearing clothes of English fashion."[2]

On July 27, 1813 immediately following the War of 1812, Norton wed Catherine Munn (also known as Maus, Mons or perhaps Docherty; her native name was Karighwaycagh), a sixteen year old Native woman. They were married by Reverend Robert Addison in Niagara. Catherine

The farm manager's house, where Robert Thomson would have lived, was built in the early 1800's near Hillhouse. This house is all that remains of the estate.

had been brought up by her grandmother along the Grand River. Her father was said to have been white. Norton took Catherine and his ten year old son John from a previous marriage, to Dunfermline, Scotland where they attended school in the care of Mr. and Mrs. Johnstone, friends from Norton's own hometown. Young John was to stay to complete his schooling while Catherine returned to Canada with her husband in 1817.

That year Captain Norton promised Reverend Robert Addison, the Anglican missionary with the Church of England to Niagara and the Indians at Six Nations, that he would translate the gospels of the Bible into Mohawk. Although he had completed the translation of St. Matthew by 1821, he was worried that the rest would be of little use and did not complete the task. Later Aaron Hill and Dr. John Strachan would finish the work begun by Norton.

Over the years Norton had acquired a large tract of land of about 925 acres overlooking the Grand River below Caledonia which we know today as the area of Sims Lock. This is where Hillhouse was built for him and his wife. The farm manager's small log house still remains as a reminder of its history. Today, the road (Highway 54) is to the south of the log house. However, when Hillhouse was just a few feet west of the log house, the road ran north of the house. It was here that the duel was to be fought.

The story of the so-called 'Last Duel in Canada' begins when Norton's life took an unfortunate turn at hay-making time in 1823.[3] His debts had been increasing to the degree that the Third Duke of Northumberland had paid for young John's education. Depressed by his lack of funds and his corresponding inability to travel, he was growing restless and feeling limited in his role as farmer. Over the years he had enjoyed being a celebrity, called upon to verify war records of Indians and settlers and recommended by influential friends to those seeking advice. Now his life was restricted and confining.

One day Catherine complained to her husband of a young man making advances to her. The distraught Norton abruptly sent notice for both of them to leave the area. The Champlain Society published word for word, John Norton's own account of the incident as written in a letter to his friend, Colonel John Harvey, a veteran of the War of 1812. He began by saying an unfortunate affair had occurred at his place that had filled his heart with vexation and grief. The young man his wife had complained about was Joseph Big Arrow, a person Norton had affectionately fostered from childhood.

Neither individual had obeyed Norton's notice. When the young man came to the house, Catherine rushed downstairs and accused him to his face, "upbraiding my moderation", said Norton.[4] He didn't exactly remember what he said, but he knew he felt angry yet reluctant to hurt him. When the young man dared Norton, Norton told him to choose his weapons, noting in his letter that the young man should have an equal chance. As he took his pistol and prepared it, Norton noted that there were several people standing by.

"I told him that when he took aim at me and I saw him ready to fire I would treat him as I did my enemies – he advanced taking the rising ground on one side until within three paces, when he presented at my head: after firing, it appears he sprung upon me: and had seized or in some manner changed the direction of the pistol for the ball passed downward and through his thigh, while his ball grazed the top of my head." This Norton described in the letter.[5]

According to the trial transcripts, Joseph Big Arrow of Bearfoot Village on the Grand River, died about forty-eight hours later. Witnesses were reported to have said that Norton lamented at what had happened and was heard to say, "Oh, my Joseph."[6]

His letter expressed his ongoing feelings of pity and distress and identified that on the third day friends told him he should leave home in anticipation of a change of situation which might afford relief of mind. He told Colonel Harvey that he had written to the Attorney General offering himself for trial, naming as many witnesses as he had remembered. He also stated that he was going to take a young Cherokee friend to his country where he would remain for the winter, a trip he had been wanting to take.

Although Norton had not named the young man he had challenged to a duel, his son John, by this time a young man himself, in writing to his father to tell him to leave because of the families' embitterment, indicated that the fellow's English name was Crawford. John had also proposed that a settlement be made to the injured family as it was an Indian custom.

Following his trial in Niagara, Norton described the proceedings for Colonel Harvey saying he had been kept in prison until the verdict was announced; a fine of twenty-five pounds. Big Arrow, (Joe Crawford) had left a widow and two children. He noted that Big Arrow's pension might be allowed to continue to his family for a little time.

Norton refused to see his wife. Catherine wrote to him on August 3, 1823 pleading that he not believe all that people were saying against her. She had left with only a blanket. A trunk had been sent to her later with many things taken out. She said she had heard they wanted to kill her, but that she believed it was all false. She wrote, "God forgive me my sins, I will never forget it all the days of my life."[7] She ended by saying she hoped Norton would not forsake her all together and asked again for his forgiveness.

There is evidence to conclude, according to *The Journal,* that Norton had directed his pension to Catherine, with the last payment made on February 25, 1826. There is also evidence to conclude that Catherine went to Moraviantown on the Thames River which is in the St. Thomas area of today. She died January 16, 1827.

The *Niagara Gleaner* printed the account of the trial on September 20, 1823. It said Norton would no doubt have been acquitted altogether if he had not, from feelings of delicacy, withheld his best defense.

Norton left for Cherokee country following the trial, where it is believed he lived until his death in October 1831. Hillhouse Farm was looked after by the farm manager, Robert Thomson, until 1838 when Charles Bain purchased the land from the government. The surrender document, which the Bain family still have in their possession, is signed by forty Indian Chieftains. The money from the sale went into a fund on which the Indians drew interest. The original home burned in 1838 and in 1840 the present house was built.

John Norton Jr. returned to Canada to live on the Huff Tract near Cayuga where he had received a patent from the Crown for 388 acres. On August 3, 1840 he sold this property and moved to Thamesville.

A memorial to Captain John Norton was placed in a stained glass window of the historic Mohawk Chapel in Brantford where it can be seen to this day. The inscription reads, "installed with the gracious approval of Her Majesty Queen Elizabeth II to commemorate the special association for the Chapel of the Mohawks with the Royal Family. Dedicated on May 27, 1962, the 250th anniversary of the gift of a Bible 'To Her Majesty's Chapel for the Mohawks' by Queen Anne in 1712, this window portrays the distribution of the Gospels in Mohawk in 1806."

"Let us strictly adhere to what our Lord has transmitted to us in the Holy Scriptures, that thereby the unbelievers may know the love we bear the commandments of God. Preface to St. John's Gospel – Captain John Norton."

By River and Rail

Navigation on the Grand River

The Grand River Navigation system began full operation in 1835. In all the Company had built five locks and five dams, with three more locks and a dam at Brantford to be completed in 1848. Local resources of timber, gravel and stone were used in the construction. Built to last, the lock walls were about six feet thick at the base and five feet at the top.

In 1834, S.H. Farnsworth and Jacob Turner were advertising: "two to three hundred steady labouring men will find constant employment on the Grand River Canal. To carpenters and masons as well as common labourers, industrious and faithful workmen, liberal wages will be given through the season, either by the day, month or job. No spirituous liquors will be allowed on or near the work."[8] Soon quantities of timber, barley, wheat, liquor and salt pork were making their way down the river.

The great timber rafts played a vital role in the economic life of the river. Timber intended for European markets was piled at riverside mills during the winter and at spring freshet time rafted downstream, pike-poled and prodded or pulled by donkeys, oxen or horses walking along the bank.

By 1846 there were 566 scows and barges passing through the Grand River Canal. The tugboats, *Jessie* and *Swallow*, often pulled, pushed or nudged the flat-bottomed, wide-waisted unattractive scows along the waterway. In addition to the scows, 312 steamboats passed through the locks. The passenger steamships *Brantford* and the *Caroline Messmore* cruised the river with high-pressure steam engines producing a speed of 5 knots. Ranald McKinnon, in one of his letters, said, "Neither of these boats have the speed necessary to make them useful here."[9] Seven years later this traffic had more than doubled.

However, the belles of the Grand River were the schooners, the full-skirted and proud vessels of their time. After the Brantford cut was opened in 1848, a line of sailing ships operated on a regular basis. The *Tuscarora*, *Onondaga* and *Mohawk* graced the river as they passed downstream in succession, bound from one inland port to another.

While in its prime, this period of navigation was probably the most colourful portion of the history of the Grand River. Passenger boats, like the well-known *Red Jacket* steamship, and the monarch of them all, *The Queen*, were small replicas of the Mississippi stern wheelers. *The Queen*, registered in 1851, carried about 40 passengers and boasted two good staterooms and excellent meals. It is said the crew consisted of a master, a mate, one engineer, two firemen, two wheelmen, two deck hands, a cook, steward, stewardess and purser.

By 1849 extensive profits allowed an increase in the capital stock of the Company. However, by 1853 a report confirmed that the emergence of railway lines would likely lead to the less bulky items being gradually drawn away from the boats. Indeed, during the period from 1854-60, an aura of doom was falling on the navigation company. By April 1871, it had passed out of existence and was sold to the Haldimand Navigation Company, who abandoned all the dams except the one at York. Only the freight boats *Caledonia* and *Port Dover* were still in service until the early 1860's.

The collapse of the Grand River Navigation Company meant that huge sums of money were lost, including a considerable amount which had been invested by the Receiver General of Canada on behalf of the Six Nations Indians. Thus a portion of the money credited to them when the government took over the Grand River Grant in 1832 was gone forever.

Indiana, situated between York and Cayuga, became a ghost town. By 1851 its founder, David Thompson (Member of Parliament from 1841-1851), had died and the demise of the Grand River Navigation Company sent inhabitants to other villages. David Thompson's large mansion "Ruthven", constructed in 1845, was all that was left of Indiana by the turn of the century. Ruthven and its in excess of 1,200 acre estate remained in the family until the fifth generation David Thompson died in August, 1993. Today, the estate is attracting wide interest as the Lower Grand River Trust Foundation and the Ruthven Management Committee develops and restores Ruthven Park, as a living memorial to David Thompson and his family for their contribution to settlement in Haldimand County.

Ruthven Mansion sits on a 1,600-acre estate known as Ruthven Park on Highway 54 between York and Cayuga, not far from Caledonia. It was acquired by the Lower Grand River Land Trust Foundation in May 1994 to be developed and preserved as a memorial to the Thompson family. The mansion was begun in 1844 by David Thompson (1793-1851) during the heyday of the Grand River Navigation System. John Latchaw of Niagara was hired as the architect. Ruthven is one of the best examples of Greek Classical Revivalist architecture in North America. Since it was built it has been owned by the Thompson family: David Thompson's son David, until 1886; Colonel Andrew Thompson, until 1939; Andrew Thompson's grandsons, Andrew (1992) and David, until his death in 1993. Ruthven is undergoing extensive renovations in preparation for public viewing.

A replica of the *Red Jacket* crafted for the 1967 Centennial Parade in Caledonia.

In February 1994, the Grand River was designated as a Canadian Heritage River. It is considered one of the oldest rivers in Ontario with its outstanding geology resulting from landforms created by the last glaciation 12,000 years ago. The Grand River flows through more than 60 municipalities in the most densely populated part of Canada. It is 290 kilometres long from its mouth at Port Maitland to its source in Dufferin County. The heritage designation includes its four major tributaries, the Nith, Conestoga, Speed and Eramosa.

The Grand River's industrial heritage is recognized for its outstanding human heritage resources. The strong association of Native Peoples with the watershed for thousands of years is also represented in the formal designation. Grand River communities like Caledonia are committed to ensuring that heritage and recreational resources are maintained and enhanced for future generations.

Transportation on the Rails

For Caledonia, the advent of the railroad meant the beginning of the end for navigation on the Grand River. This first railway known as the Buffalo, Brantford and Goderich, linked Buffalo on the Niagara River to Caledonia. The Paris Junction and the Great Western Railway continued the line connecting Caledonia to Goderich on Lake Huron.

When this Buffalo to Lake Huron railway went through Caledonia in 1852, the community's steady population growth came to a halt. Equal numbers of people moving in and out of town stabilized the population at 1,250 until 1881. Then the population began to decline until it reached its lowest level of 801 in 1901. However, by 1941, Caledonia had regained its population and was once again a thriving community consisting of 1401 people.

The mid-nineteenth century was a time of new development. Despite a fire which destroyed the best of the business section in 1862, private enterprise continued to invest and rebuild businesses despite the fact that the debt load to the town council of $40,000 for the building of the Hamilton Port Dover line delayed much needed sidewalks and services.

During the 1860's and 1870's, factories such as Ranald McKinnon's woollen factory (built in 1863), the Scott Foundry, and Shoots and Avery Carrieage Shop (manufacturers of wagons, buggies and fancy horse vehicles) were doing big business. For a time, Caledonia became the centre of an extensive square timber and sawed lumber trade, much of which was shipped by barge along the Grand River waterway. However, as the vast timber resources diminished, the lumber trade gradually tapered off. Now that much of the land had been cleared, farming began to appear more attractive to settlers.

Although it took some time for manufacturing and agriculture to switch over to rail travel, there was a gradual transition during the 50's. The river was still being used in the early 1870's to transport gypsum from York to Caledonia, where it was hauled by team and wagon to the train

At one time steam engines were seen often at the Caledonia station.

station and shipped by rail to Paris for processing. In March 1866 a petition was passed by the village council so that all day express trains were ordered to stop in Caledonia. This increase in rail service made it more convenient for Simcoe and Port Dover people to use the trains rather than the Grand River Navigation system.

The town's people and businesses were anticipating great things with the construction of the new Hamilton Port Dover line. Of course, in the end, this was illusionary because it not only took twenty years, from 1854 – 1878 to complete, but it never became the great railway divisional point as promised. The canal system on the Great Lakes was being constantly improved and additional railroads were being built from Western Ontario to the level of Lake Ontario.

By 1863, the town had sunk $40,000 into the venture and Hamilton had committed $500,000 more. The rail bed had been graded and was ready for ties and rails from Hamilton to Caledonia, but the need for more money brought construction to a standstill. In addition to the delays, the huge cost had halted, to the dismay of many, other much needed public works in the community.

Finally, in 1873 the line was completed. The wooden railroad bridge across the Grand River had been built at last. On June 30th, amid much celebration, the wood-burning John Scott locomotive, from the local foundry, pulled the first express train through to Jarvis. Mr. McLean was the watchman on this wooden bridge. He would make an inspection walk across the length of the structure after each train passed over. Barrels of water were placed along the bridge as a safety precaution against fire. This bridge was replaced in 1886 with a solid deck reconstruction.

With the railroad came a flurry of activity. The Campbell House Hotel was built near the railroad tracks on the site where a Tim Hortons stands today: this structure would burn down in 1931. Increased passengers meant increased business for many including livery stables. Often a fine team of black horses pulling a surrey would be seen taxiing rail passengers from the station to the downtown Union Hotel.

Did this rail line live up to its projected affect on the growth of Caledonia? Certainly the canal system on the Great Lakes was improved and additional railroads were built. Yet the heavy debt and the holding back of public works in Caledonia was problematic. The Hamilton to Port Dover line was blamed for any village misfortune although its real affect did not become evident until years later. It was claimed that if the

Surrey at Union Hotel waiting to taxi customers from hotel to train station in the late 1880's.

Hamilton line had not gone through Caledonia, the village might have declined to the same level of insignificance of other villages that no longer exist today.

Why was Caledonia different from most Ontario villages that showed an increase of population in the years following the advent of railroads? The advent of the railroad did not add to the prosperity of Caledonia as largely as was anticipated. The railway drew business from the Grand River Navigation Company which had worked up a great and thriving business. The railroad destroyed the village's comparative position of being situated on one of the only good inland water systems in Southwestern Ontario.

Despite the consequences of competition between the river and rail industries, over the years the train made many major contributions to the community, in time earning a special place in the hearts of Caledonians. Jessie MacGregor's Concert Bureau certainly made use of the rail service to transport her entourage of entertainers to centres all over Ontario. Deals were made with Passenger Associations for the Old Boys and Old Girls Reunion in 1927. Reduced fares were arranged on the train from all points in Canada where fares were more than 75 cents. A certificate

ARGYLE ST., CALEDONIA, ONT.

A Gorman & Co. postcard, printed in Germany, of the main street looking south to the bridge at the turn of the century.

would entitle all passengers to return at one-half regular fare. If tickets couldn't be procured to Caledonia from agents, passengers were told to get a ticket to Hamilton and transfer from there to Caledonia. However, special fares were not available to those coming from the United States.

Thousands came to Caledonia's Fair every year taking the train from Hamilton. When the Fair's midway came into town on the train, it was taken by team and wagon to the fairgrounds. There were weigh scales on the Dennis Kelly farm, now known as the Bob Thompson farm, where farmers would bring their stock to be weighed and transferred into the nearby stockyard in readiness for shipment by rail to Hamilton. Dennis Kelly was a buyer for the Kohler Bros. of Cayuga in the 1930's and 40's. On a Monday morning one would see twenty teams of horses and wagons at the weigh scales waiting for the train.

Entertainment for young children in the 1920's was sitting by the railroad track to watch the trains go by. They were coming and going constantly during those years. However, the days when you might see six big steam engines go through on a Sunday afternoon were gone by the 1950's.

Today trains entering Caledonia are from Brantford. There is none that goes east beyond the town. When a train arrives in town these days, residents listen for how long and hard its whistle blows. The three short runs a day, from Brantford to Caledonia and crossing the railway bridge enroute to Nanticoke, keep the train whistle alive in Caledonia.

The Caledonia station, built in 1913, was closed as a parcel depot in November, 1977. Until its total closure in 1982, it was used for a maintenance and storage depot. Although the building had been approved for demolition it remained standing and was used as a tool house. Today it is boarded up. There is active community interest in having the station designated as a heritage building, restored and put to good use as a tourist information centre.

Carrying the mail from the train station to the Post Office early 1900's.

The Caledonia railway station was built in 1913 and remains as a reminder of the days of a crowded platform and busy train travel.

Caledonia Fair

Since October 15, 1873, the smells and sounds of fair time have symbolized the beginning of fall in Caledonia. The first fair was held on Edinburgh Square. Five years later, on July 17, 1878, the Caledonia Agricultural and Arts Society purchased the present fairgrounds, well-located within the town, from the Dominion Government for two-hundred and fifty dollars. That year there was a two-day fair held on October 16 and 17.

Fairs in the old county of Haldimand were held many years before 1873 when they were sponsored by the Niagara District Agricultural Society, founded in 1832. The Haldimand Agricultural Society was formed in 1843

Horse racing was once a feature of the Caledonia Fair. In its day the landmark grandstand, moved from Hamilton Central Fairgrounds in 1898, was filled to capacity for afternoon racing.

Caledonia Fair before the turn of the century shows a midway as busy as it is today.

when the first grant of five pounds came from the Governor General.

The villages of Seneca and Oneida, Seneca to the east and Oneida to the west of Caledonia, both held fairs alternating years and in 1854 the Seneca and Oneida Agricultural Society was thriving, according to earliest records. It had 218 members and a bank balance of fifty pounds.

In January 1873, the Caledonia Agricultural and Arts Society held its first meeting in the Town Hall when a board of thirty-two directors was established. Captain Hugh Stewart was President, Robert Shirra was secretary and Robert Hudspeth held the position of treasurer.

Queen Victoria's sixty-year reign was celebrated in 1867 at the Caledonia Fair. That year, log-sawing contests and three bicycle races were staged. Even a heaviest baby contest limited to infants under 18 months old was held. However, this contest was protested by a Mrs. Patterson who won the appeal.

In 1907, a total of 11,400 people registered at what they called the Great Fair when there was a gathering of Haldimand "old boys and girls". Special trains were run from all directions for Caledonia Fair and as many as twenty-thousand paid admission during some of those years.

The exhibition hall at Caledonia Fair in 1950 was said to be one of the best in the province. It still carries that distinction.

Women Directors were invited to participate and attend the Annual Banquet of the Society in 1913. These annual functions were held in February during full moon so out-of-town members could see their way home.

There were 16,000 people who paid admission in 1913. According to a report from the local daily, *The Hamilton Spectator*, quoted in the *Grand River Sachem*, it took from 5:30 p.m. Saturday when the grounds were vacated until close to midnight to transport everyone on the Caledonia railway station platform. Trains coming in and departing Caledonia for Hamilton were loaded two or three times before the last three hundred boarded an extra run at 11:00 that night.

It was also in July 1913 when Joseph Hudspeth, one of the oldest directors of the Caledonia Agricultural Society, was presented with a cane by the society. Mr. Hudspeth had not been well for some time and his fellow directors decided some support to keep mobile. Joseph Hudspeth died August 13, 1913.

By 1928 a three-day fair was held, but the polio epidemic in 1937 was reason enough to cancel that year's fair, the only year when a fall fair was not held in Caledonia.

Over the years Caledonia Fair has grown with the times. Excitement fills the air for young and old alike as much today as it did in 1873. Held in the last weekend of September on the beautifully kept fair grounds along the banks of the Grand River, the Fair continues to attract thousands of people. For many years the Caledonia Fair's exhibit hall has been proudly recognized as one of the best in the province.

The Incurable Optimist

By 1846, just 11 years after Ranald McKinnon first arrived in this wilderness area, Caledonia was booming. The dam was built, the river was busy transporting goods and people, the plank road was open for traffic from Hamilton to Port Dover, a swing bridge allowed for easy travel across the river and streets and squares were named.

What had been Seneca Village to the east and Oneida Village to the west on the north side of the river were now part of the village of Caledonia. The other nearby small residential areas of Sunnyside and South Seneca Village were not yet included. For some time the village of Oneida was nicknamed Little Caledonia, while the village of Seneca retained its original name for specific referral.

What in 1835 had been no more than Mr. Bryant's tavern on the

Ranald McKinnon, founder of Caledonia

north east corner with the two adjacent log houses, by 1846 consisted of a physician's residence, five stores, three taverns, two grocery stores, two wagon-makers, two cabinet-makers, three blacksmiths, three shoemakers, three tailors and two bakers. Ranald McKinnon's saw and grist mills and Jacob Turner's saw mill would, in 1850, be joined by McKinnon's woollen mill. Some three hundred people were residing and working in Caledonia with more arriving each day.

Born in Ardelum on the Isle of Mull, Argyleshire, Scotland on Sep-

tember 11, 1801, Ranald McKinnon was just four years old when his family emigrated to Masonville, New York. In 1820 the family moved to
Esquising, not far from Streetsville in Canada. At age twenty-four Ranald
was employed in building the Rideau Canal. By the time he left in 1832 he
had established a reputation of achievement in the construction field. In
1835 he was commissioned as a contractor on dam and lock number five
for the Grand River Navigation Company. It was McKinnon who pushed
to have the bridge built in the location it now stands, a legacy to his foresight. Otherwise the bridge might have been built at the Seneca Village area.

McKinnon's ability to remain in the public eye was rewarded once
again when he was contracted, in 1845, to build the portion of the plank
road from Hagersville to Port Dover, thus completing the earlier link
from Hamilton Mountain to Hagersville. By this time McKinnon's efforts
and acquisitions were increasing his wealth. It was McKinnon who had
land or housing to either sell or rent to the Mill workers needing housing
for their families. He had positioned himself well.

It is not surprising that McKinnon was also becoming interested in
politics. About 1846 he was petitioned to run for political office by residents of the community who felt they needed a local representative familiar with the needs of the area. The tradition of someone from Toronto
whose main interest was to "act" in parliament was losing favour. In 1851
he ran for the Haldimand seat against William Lyon McKenzie and
George Brown. This was a hard-fought by-election held to fill the va-
cancy left by David Thompson's death. Despite the local petitions
McKinnon lost by a few votes to William Lyon MacKenzie of Toronto.

There were four general elections from 1851 to 1858. In the first three,
McKinnon ran for the Conservative party and lost to the "Little Mac".
In his fourth and last effort in 1858, MacKinnon dropped out at the last
minute, perhaps avoiding what might have been another defeat.

During the 1870's the once wealthy mill owner was having severe financial problems. Many properties he owned had to be sold under the
Insolvent Act. His grist and woollen mills had burned down in the fifties
and again in the sixties. The rebuilding had required considerable expense. However, by 1873 McKinnon found his place in local politics. He
was back as Reeve and was still the optimist despite his earlier setbacks.

In 1875 he initiated the construction of a steel bridge on the original
site to replace the initial wooden structure. That structure would remain
until 1927 when the present bridge was built.

Squire McKinnon, the politician, speaking to crowds at the train station.

By the time Ranald McKinnon died in 1879, a handsome village and community had evolved from an area that had been dense with bush and wilderness only forty-four years earlier. His vision and efforts against numerous odds led to his being known as the "Incurable Optimist" and the founder of Caledonia.

The McKinnon Lifestyle

The Ranald McKinnon home still stands today at 232 Caithness St. West, overlooking the dam. For almost a century it remained in the family, but once sold it gradually fell into relative obscurity, its historical significance all but forgotten.

Ranald, 34 years old when he came to work on the dam in 1835, was married in March of that same year to his cousin, Euphemia McKinnon from Masonville, New York. Euphemia was just 22 years old at the time.

The McKinnons had nine children. Malcolm, Donald, Mary and Catherine died shortly after birth. Christina, Isobella, Flora, Archibald and John survived and the McKinnon household prospered. Soon Ranald was known as Squire McKinnon to separate him from other

McKinnons living nearby. Besides his sons there were Neil, a nephew and Dr. Ranald, a son of Neil.

Stories passed down by persons who knew the family and who visited in the home in their youth describe the McKinnon family as living in a gracious manner. As they became more prosperous the original log home was torn down and a large new home with an east and west wing was built on the same property. The east wing contained the drawing room while the west wing, with a separate entrance, was Ranald's office. Above his office were the servants' quarters. To the rear of the west wing, there was a coach house with room for two coaches. Later this would become the garage. The main house, without the wings, had fourteen rooms.

In 1842 Ranald McKinnon was identified as a merchant engaged in trade and commerce as well as owner of the sawmill. He had a store at the northwest corner of Argyle and Caithness St. listed under the name of his good friend John Scott & Co., to keep it separate from his mills. He owned 40 acres described as occupied and 70 acres listed as improved. Records show that in one year he produced 40 bushels of wheat and 150 bushels of potatoes and that he had 7 cattle, 3 horses, 8 sheep, 7 hogs and 20 pounds of wool. He also had three servants.[10]

The McKinnons, active Presbyterians, supported the building of the first Presbyterian Church in 1849. Their Sabbath School Picnic of 1859 was held at Squire McKinnon's grove on his farm. He had placed tables, benches and swings on the grounds to accommodate about 80 children plus a large number of adults. It is likely that there were many such events held at his home.

When he ran in his last campaign in 1858, the publisher of the *Grand River Sachem*, known to be a Conservative newspaper, said, "Mr. McKinnon is not only well known throughout the county but possesses a name in every part of Upper Canada as an extensive manufacturer and merchant, a gentleman of more than ordinary abilities as a practical business man, and just such a one is required at this time to study and carry out the wishes of an agricultural and manufacturing community such as ours."[11]

By 1861, the Ranald McKinnon household included four carriages for pleasure, with an acre of land attached to the house. His business, still expanding, consisted of merchandising, milling, farming and lumbering. He annually employed an average of twenty-five men and two women.

The properties just east of the home at 194-196 Caithness Street and at 192 Caithness Street West were also owned by Ranald McKinnon. Both these homes still stand. The one at 192 Caithness was built in 1860 for his eldest son, John, who later sold it to his brother Archibald for $2,000. John had acquired it from his father for $1,700.

John and his wife Sophia (Matthews), an accomplished musician, played a major role in the life of Caledonia. John, who owned a dry goods store in the village, became the Reeve on three different occasions. Little is known of Archibald other than he attended military school.

In 1871, just eight years before Ranald's death, the saw mill was worth $1,000 while his woollen factory had a fixed capital of $31,000 and the grist and flouring mill had a fixed capital of $9,000.

Ranald died on October 18, 1879 in his seventy-ninth year. His wife, Euphemia, was to live for another sixteen years. She died April 30, 1895 in her eighty-third year.

After her mother died, Christina lived in part of the big house until she married Laughlan McQuarrie in May of 1906. A local beekeeper, Henry Pedlow who lived in one room of the house until 1921, said it still contained the tapestries and furnishings that belonged to the McKinnon's. Included in these furnishings were a grand piano and a set of chairs.

A granddaughter, Effie Eadie, daughter of Flora (McKinnon) Eadie of Allanhurst, New Jersey, sold the property in 1926 to Walter Carpenter who owned it until 1940. During the hurricane in 1936 the roof blew off the house showing rafters, of four by four pine and the square-cut nails

Although the dam he built has been replaced since it was first constructed, the McKinnon home has withstood all test of time. Today it no longer commands the attention it once did when it was known as the Squire McKinnon's estate home on the hill. Yet through the careful maintenance of its former and present owners, the home remains as an enduring remembrance of Caledonia's founder.

James Little

It is said by some that James Little was as much a founder of Caledonia as was Ranald McKinnon. Little's development of the south side of the river is reason enough for the statement.

At the same time that Caledonia was getting its start, so was the village of Seneca. With a year's head start on Caledonia, it claimed about 250 residents. Some predicted it would be the main residential area rather than

Caledonia. In 1837 further development seemed likely when The Grand River Navigation Company obtained a grant of 368.7 acres at Seneca Hill.

However, by 1846 Seneca was a village with only 140 residents, a saw mill on both banks, a grist mill, a wool carding mill, a sash and door factory, a Methodist church, a log schoolhouse, a chair factory and a physician. The population declined as residents were moving to the Caledonia village.

Among those businesses in Seneca was a store run by James Little, the first postmaster of the village. Although he was still in business in 1846 in Seneca, he had purchased considerable land on the south side of the river in anticipation of a bridge and plank road that would extend south to link with Caledonia.

Little's first and oldest existing building is the historic landmark Haldimand House. Completed in 1842, the building's history began in 1836 when Haldimand County issued License No. 1 for a stage coach inn. In 1867, the James Little Estate sold it to the Sutherland family who owned it for four years and then sold to Bridget Britton. James Hayes purchased Haldimand House in 1875. Then, in 1900 it passed into the possession of the Matthew Richardson family estate. Today Haldimand House is an apartment complex. Owner Louis Leousis, and his son Chris, have plans to restore the building in an attempt to recapture some its early grandeur when it was an inn famous for its ciders.

James Little began construction on Haldimand House in 1836. It still stands today.

The Ryan House in the early 1900's. Reading right to left, first man unidentified, Jack Murphy, brother of Belle Murphy, Bert Mellish, "Bolt" Ryan, last man unidentified. Haldimand House is on the left.

The plank road envisioned by James Little is now Highway 6. Completed in 1844, it runs from Port Dover to the top of Hamilton Mountain. With its construction completed, Caledonia forged ahead of Seneca Village and Little's Post Office and store were moved to the south side.

Another landmark building, built by James Little in the early 1850's and which still stands today, is the Caledonia Mill. It was first known as the Balmoral Mill, later as the Grand River Mills and eventually became The Caledonia Milling Company.

James Little went on to construct more homes on land he owned. One of those was the first brick home of the area, built in 1855 at 20 Wigton Street. He also erected a hotel across the street from Haldimand House, at the southwest corner of the bridge. In 1870, this property was sold to William Munro and later to John Ryan when it became known as the popular Ryan Hotel or Mansion House. Today it is owned by Mary Mellish.

An ambitious entrepreneur and an influential contractor, James Little used his position to ensure that the Hamilton and Port Dover Railway would run through Caledonia rather than Cayuga. As a director of the railway line and holder of stock valued at 100 pounds, his influence led to the town's making a 10,000 pound (equivalent to about forty thousand dollars) commitment to the line. That railway was not completed until 1873, at great expense of the local populace.

Originally from Londonderry, Northern Ireland, James Little and his wife Ann had seven children. The eldest, John, was born in 1832. Besides John, there were William, Charles, Leonard, Margaret Jane, Harriet and James. Margaret Jane married the Hon. Edmond Spring Rice and lived in Montreal. William went on to become President of the Canadian Forestry Association.

In 1867 Little's holdings went to Thomas Cockburn Kerr of Hamilton and were later sold to Wm. Munro who also became a partner in Balmoral Mill. James Little died in Montreal in his eightieth year, October 2, 1883.

William Moore

If James Little was responsible for the development of Caledonia south of the river, William Moore was responsible for the Caledonia development north of Orkney Street, south and north of the railroad tracks, but east of today's Highway 6.

William Moore came to Caledonia from Londonderry, Northern Ireland in 1840. He was just twenty-seven years old. His first home, on the northeast corner of Highway 6 and Orkney St. E., was constructed to resemble his family home, "Barnfoot", in Londonderry. There he lived with his mother and sister, Elizabeth.

In 1850 William and Elizabeth bought one hundred acres from the Crown and built numerous homes along Orkney Street, many are still there today. One, at 96 Orkney St. E., was assembled according to a design of a sea captain who wished a particular look-out room on the roof.

The farm home just north of the railroad tracks, now owned by Bob and Helen Thompson, was also built by William Moore. In 1852 he sold the right of way for the railway to cut through this property. He also owned and developed a farm on a piece of land west of Caledonia, formerly known as the Williamson farm.

A Number 1 Lucerne seed imported from Scotland in 1881 that yielded one bushel per acre in its first year became known as Moore's seed, and is still grown on the farm by Bob Thompson.

Although a lifelong bachelor, William Moore was an active community member. Along with Ranald McKinnon he helped found the Presbyterian Church and became its first treasurer. Upon his death in 1868 he left the estate to his nephew, William Henry Moore. This nephew was killed in the first year of his marriage leaving his widow, the daughter of William Marston, a Caledonia storekeeper, and their infant son named William Henry Marston Moore. The estate was administered until William came of age. William Henry Marston Moore received the deed for the property in 1912. He sold it in 1914.

Well Loved and Remembered

The Good Old Days of the Opera House

There are few memories that bring more pleasure than those of the days of the Opera House. The people who remember talk of its past with fondness.

Known also as the Roper Block, the Opera House was built in the 1850's by Mr. Bryant, the same Mr. Bryant who owned the tavern Ranald McKinnon came upon when he first came to the area. The Roper Block was built on the property at the northeast corner of Argyle and Caithness Streets. It was a magnificent structure and with three storeys it was the largest building in Haldimand County.

The three-storey Opera House (1850's to 1947) is a dominant landmark in this late 1880's street scene.

The Opera House fire in June of 1947.

The lower floor held stores of business: a barber shop, F. Simpson Variety Store, M.E. Forster Variety, the Roper Drug Store, the Bank of Hamilton and others. The second floor contained the huge concert hall with the Harrison Arrell Barrister office occupying one end from 1905 to 1932. The third floor was a lodge hall for the St. Andrews Lodge and the Caledonia Chapter 236.

Vaudeville shows, Chautauqua shows and other travelling road shows entertained in the Opera House, attracting crowds from a wide area. One person remembered, as a small boy, attending a performance of the week-long roadshow production of "Uncle Tom's Cabin". For many, it is the big band ballroom dances which hold the fondest and richest memories. It was a common occurrence to break up a chair to re-kindle the fire when it was necessary. It was also common knowledge that the vibration from dancing knocked items from the shelves of the variety store below. Rods were finally strung across the ceiling of the basement to cut down the impact created by the enthusiastic dancers.

Election times found the opera hall much in demand. This was by far the best place to see and hear the political party leaders. Huge Haldimand County crowds came in droves to support or revile the leaders of the day.

St. Paul's Anglican Church held a celebration for its 75th Anniversary in the Opera House on January 25th, 1926. Four hundred people sat down to dinner in the concert hall, all decorated in pink and green. In the centre of the head table stood a five storey birthday cake, illuminated by seventy-five pink candles, a special occasion for Caledonia.

The Opera House was destroyed by fire in June, 1947. The estimated damage from the fire that brought an end to both an important landmark and social era was claimed to be $125,000. Citizens of all ages were on hand to view the spectacular blaze, many still in their night attire, helpless in the face of the all consuming blaze.

The era of the Opera House in Caledonia was never to be repeated. A two storey building with apartments on the second floor was built at the same location in 1950.

A "Lovable" Constable

Known as the "lovable" Constable, Bill Stotts was revered by all who knew him. The small child he would call by name and take across the street was as important to the Constable as were his Six Nations friends he would drive home if they needed a ride.

People who remember Bill Stotts say he was gentle, kind and courageous. At the same time, they say, he was firm. The respect he held for his fellow man came back to him a hundred fold. The Six Nations visitors responded to his kindness by assisting him in controlling any troublemakers. He used discretion, not force. However, if force were needed, he had a grip like a vice. There was no question as to who was in control.

Constable Stotts and his wife lived on the main floor of the Town Hall from 1937 to 1955. The jail in the basement was no longer in use. All lock-ups by this time had to be transported to the Cayuga jail.

Stotts worked alone, always on 24-hour duty. As well as the policeman for the community, he was the dog catcher, sold dog licences and returned the lost dogs and stray cats he found to worried owners.

One story is told of three hoodlums who were

The "Lovable" Constable William Stotts.

about to speed away in a stolen car when Constable Stotts stood in front of the car with his arms out. They were handcuffed and arrested on the spot.

The traffic director for the town as well, he never missed the duty expected for a funeral procession. His lookout point was a small office on the corner of Argyle and Caithness street, a spot provided by a merchant where he could be inside yet able to keep his eye on the town streets.

When the big storm of 1945 hit Caledonia, the roads were blocked from all directions. One night during the extended blizzard, a baby decided to be born. The distraught parents, unable to get their car out of the garage, appealed to Constable Stotts for help. At five in the morning, despite all the hazards, he was able to rescue mother from the house and get her to the hospital over treacherous roads. In keeping with his style, he refused to take a cent, only too happy to help. For him this gesture was an expected part of the job.

He was dependable, trusted and a friend to all. Those who remember say Caledonia is a better place, because for a time Bill Stotts was its protector. He died in 1959 mourned by many. His wife Ann was remarried to W.E. Elliott of Goderich, Ontario and in 1993 celebrated her one hundredth birthday in Goderich.

The MacGregor Concert Bureau

The MacGregor Concert Bureau, an entertainment business in Caledonia, was well known throughout Ontario during the 1920's, 30's and 40's. Jessie Cameron MacGregor, a native of Caledonia, was one of Donald and Jean MacGregor's six children. The family owned a hardware and insurance business in the town.

Jessie, showing an early aptitude for music, studied at the Toronto Conservatory as a student of the noted Russian virtuoso of the day, Mark Hambourg. Her talent led to extensive postgraduate studies in Boston. At one time she was invited to perform on the Great Organ in the Boston Symphony Hall. By this time she had already studied with one of the world's great masters, Frank Welsman, the founder of the Toronto Symphony Orchestra and many other symphonies.

Her talent and musical encounters with the entertainers of the time, combined with an entrepreneurial bent, prompted Jessie MacGregor to set up an entertainment bureau in her hometown. Her promotional booklets featured the Bureau as the source for those committees requiring

Jessie MacGregor, a female entrepreneur for more than three decades.

entertainment from year to year. Organizations soon began to rely on Miss MacGregor as a contact person who could always be counted on to deliver the best acts available for the most reasonable price.

By 1938 Jessie had been in business for twenty years. Her long list of entertainers included vocalists, ventriloquists, dramatic readers, violinists, elocutionists, pianists, drummers, xylophone players and many others. Trios, quartets and quintets, including the Elgar Ladies, and male quartets such as The Orpheus Male Quartet were on her roster.

Personally guaranteeing every artist sent out, the MacGregor Concert Bureau simplified the work of those wishing to acquire entertainment. Brochures were sent to fair boards, garden party and church concert committees, Associations of the Eastern Star, baseball clubs, high schools, fire departments and the list went on and on.

Those on the committee would indicate the price they would pay for an anticipated entertainment, and whether or not the event would be held inside or outdoors. The MacGregor Concert Bureau would respond with a letter suggesting various combinations that might be best suited. In the majority of cases, the selection of the artists and the arranging of the programmes was left solely with the Bureau.

Jessie MacGregor (to the right of the man) and her entertainers waiting for the train at the Caledonia station.

The Bureau did not claim to handle all artists in the profession, but simply the best. First-class talent, improved service to committees and the assurance of a square deal was the reputation built by Jessie McGregor. In most cases Jessie herself personally directed the productions and played the musical accompaniment on the piano.

Numerous testimonials were sent to the Bureau following the performances and were duly printed in the Booklet of Entertainment. One such testimonial from J.D. McCallum of the Almonte Fall Fair said, "The three consecutive nights at the Almonte Fair Concerts under Miss MacGregor's direction were high-class entertainments and drew the biggest crowds in years."[12] Fire Chief A. Hilmer of Oakville said, "Our garden party draws bigger crowds each year, thanks to Miss MacGregor's excellent judgment in choosing and presenting programmes."[13] "Clean, wholesome entertainment," is how Reverend B.A. Harris, of St. Patrick's Catholic Church in Caledonia described their event.[14]

Jessie MacGregor held top honours wherever she went. Her favourite pianoforte solo, the Mendelssohn Concerto in G Minor for piano and orchestra or string quartet, was a headline performance. Her key entertainment stage in Caledonia was the July 1 annual Garden Party held on the outdoor platform constructed at the rear door of the Town Hall on Edinburgh Square. The local constable, who lived on the first floor of the building, allowed his quarters to be used for dressing rooms. Those concerts and garden parties are likely to have included Jessie MacGregor's outstanding Ladies Choir of thirty-five voices which she also organized and directed.

It was in 1925 that Ruth Rushton remembers being at a Garden Party on Edinburgh Square. She described how Jessie MacGregor walked out to the piano on the unadorned open air stage, music in hand, a faint smile on her face, her bright brown eyes taking in the audience. All of us, she recalled, sat expectantly on the pine plank seats as dusk came on.

"The long sleeveless evening dress of brocaded satin with modestly low neckline and her pleasingly plump arms seemed to emphasize her hands as they moved gracefully over the keyboard."[15] To this young public school girl, Jessie MacGregor was a vision of beauty and accomplishment as she accompanied the performers she had booked for the evening's entertainment.

"There would be a comedian, juggler, acrobat and Scottish dancers and always a good baritone singer with the Scottish accent to sing the old favourites by Harry Lauder and others."[16] Jessie MacGregor, a female entrepreneur ahead of her time, lived her life entertaining others. She was sometimes criticized for giving young talent too much stage time during a program, but she was never criticized for providing an audience for talented musicians.

Throughout these years, she successfully carried on business in a reputable fashion during the days when the competitive Chautauqua shows were high on the list of entertainment and radio and movies were just beginning to gain ground. After a long productive career, Jessie MacGregor died of a cardiac seizure on July 20, 1951.

O.T. Scott

Osborne Thomas Scott had a flare for writing poetry. His talent for rhyming verse became a unique form of promoting and reporting community events. Much of the history of Caledonia was recorded as a result of his sharp memory of people and events.

He was the son of William Scott, a mill worker for the McQuarrie (Daniel), Thorburn (James) and Munro (William) partnership that owned both mills during the 1870's. When this partnership fell into fi-

O.T. Scott (1880-1960).

nancial trouble, the Scott brothers, William and Hugh, took over the south mill while the north mill went to Robert Shirra. His father, William, organized the Caledonia Milling Company in 1892 with capital raised through shares purchased by residents of the village.

Osborne Scott, or Ob as he became known, continued to build the company. He married Alma Doughty of Ayr, Ontario and had one son. By 1929, the Caledonia Milling Company bought the north mill from Shirra and remodelled it into a feed mill. The old wooden dam was gradually replaced with a concrete dam in the mid 1930's, financed by the Caledonia Milling Company. By 1950, under Ob Scott's management and along with his son Douglas as Secretary-Treasurer, the Company realized capital of $65,000 through stock owned by ninety-five residents of the village and area.

By this time there were four places of business: a flour mill on the south side of the river, a feed mill on the north side, a feed store at the corner of Argyle and Caithness Streets and an elevator at the railway station.

The McKinnon Mill (north side of the Grand) was later owned by Robert Shirra, then was converted into a feed mill by the Caledonia Milling Co. It was abandoned by the mid-sixties and burned down in 1968.

A major landmark, The Old Mill, on the south side of the Grand, still stands today.

In 1964 the charter was surrendered and the Caledonia Milling Company, after 72 years of management by the Scott family, ceased to exist. Osborne Scott died in 1960 at the age of eighty. His wife, Alma, died shortly afterwards in 1962.

A Real Sweetheart: Eva Marlene Heddle

Caledonia's Eva Marlene Heddle made the headlines, not only in the community's own newspaper, but in other Canadian newspapers when she became Canada's Loveliest Child, the winner of a 1936 contest sponsored by the *Toronto Star*. She was just three years old when she was selected from among 11,764 other Canadian children between the ages of three and seven. A prize of $500 went with the honour, a considerable award for the time.

It was not her mother or father who had submitted the photograph, but her grandmother. Her parents were completely unaware that a very proud Grandma had entered her granddaughter in the contest until after they were advised of the win.

Reverend Norman McMillan remembers when he was called to the Caledonia Presbyterian Church in 1939. He didn't know anything about the town and asked someone about this place called Caledonia. "Oh, that's where Canada's loveliest child lives," the person replied.[17]

Canada's Loveliest Child, Marlene Heddle.

"When I arrived, who should be in our Sunday School but Marlene Heddle," said Reverend McMillan. "Her grandfather, Malcolm Heddle, had a blacksmith shop and did the ironwork on the doors of the Presbyterian Church."[18]

Eva Marlene Heddle with little memory of the big news, but only stories and pictures chronicling her activities, was not affected by the publicity that surrounded Canada's loveliest child. She grew up and became Mrs. Patrick Sullivan who today lives in Stoney Creek. The scrapbook her mother made for her tells the story.

The Rt. Honourable Arthur Meighen (1874 – 1960)

Arthur Meighen was born June 16, 1874 in Anderson, Blanchard Township, Perth County, Ontario. His first job early in life would later associate him with Caledonia and bring him there for numerous functions. History books tell us Arthur Meighen taught high school for a year after he graduated from the University of Toronto, but they don't tell us where. For the record, it was Caledonia. His first job was at Caledonia High School from 1897-1898, before he left for Winnipeg to study law. Later, in 1902 after he completed his studies, he was called to the Manitoba bar.

Meighen was first elected to the House of Commons in 1908, appointed Solicitor General in 1913, was chief draughtsman of the War-Time Elections Act and succeeded Prime Minister Borden in 1920. In 1921 his government was defeated. Once more in 1926 he was invited to form a government and this time his role as Prime Minister was even briefer, lasting for only three months.

He resigned as Conservative Leader following the Liberal victory on

September 14, 1926, but was called to the Senate on February 3, 1932 during Richard Bennett's government ministry. Eventually he became leader in the Senate. In 1935 when MacKenzie King's government took power, Meighen was Senate Opposition Leader. Meighen thus became the only person to have headed both Government and Opposition forces in both Houses of Parliament.

In 1941 he became leader of the Conservative party again, but failed in his bid to win a seat in the Commons in a federal by-election in 1942. Following this defeat, he retired from politics and resumed his law practise in Toronto.

The Rt. Honourable Arthur Meighen was seen periodically in Caledonia either as a guest for a special event or visiting with friends such as Mrs. Elizabeth Trotter and family at 100 Argyle Street, opposite the Public School. This home was sold in 1967 and later torn down to make room for the Argyle Heights Apartments.

The Grand River Sachem did not miss reporting on Arthur Meighen's successes over the years. The July 2, 1913 issue reported that he was sworn in on June 26, 1913 as Solicitor General of Canada with a salary of $5,000 a year. It also said his appointment would be a very popular one as Mr. Meighen was one of the brightest young men in the House and noted that his many friends in Caledonia congratulated him on his appointment.

Meighen came to Caledonia for two most important occasions; the 1927 Diamond Anniversary celebration and the 1950 Haldimand County Centennial Day. In his short address in 1950 he quipped, "Though I spent less than two years in Caledonia it was through circumstances beyond my control. It has been true in my life all the really important positions were of short tenure." In a more serious tone, he commented, "The tendency today of a great many people to want more and to give less is robbing them of real enjoyment."[19]

According to his students who had their own opinions of Meighen as a teacher, it was the right decision for him to turn to another vocation. It was in Caledonia, though, where his first career began and ended.

Arthur Meighen died in Toronto, August 5, 1960.

Pauline Johnson: Famous Canadian Poet

It is well-known that Pauline Johnson is as famous in the Vancouver, British Columbia area as she is in the Caledonia-Brantford-Ohsweken area of Ontario where she was born and raised. Her ashes and some of her

Emily Pauline Johnson
(Tekahionwake).

writings were buried within sight and sound of Siwash Rock in Stanley Park, B.C. A cairn was erected there in 1922 as a tribute to her from the Women's Canadian Club of Vancouver.

Her birthplace, on the Grand River in Ontario, also remains as a monument to her life and her work. Chiefswood, her home, built in 1853 and bequeathed to the Six Nations Indians in 1926, is a noted historical site and has been a museum of period artifacts since 1963.

Chiefswood is an excellent example of the classic Ontario plank-on-plank style. The mansion is located just west of Caledonia on Highway 54, along the north bank of the Grand River, overlooking the Six Nations Reserve at Ohsweken. At the turn of the century there were many visitors to Chiefswood, then recognized as the capital of Indian Canada. Numerous Tribal and Canadian leaders, as well as such dignitaries as Edward V11 and the Governor General of Canada were guests in the home of Pauline Johnson.

Pauline was born March 10, 1861 to Mohawk Chief G.H.M. Johnson, and his wife Emily Howells, originally from Bristol, England. She did not receive any formal education until age 16, but liked it best when she was by herself in the woods and fields writing poetry or paddling her canoe up and down the Grand River drinking in the beauty of nature's panorama. Some say it may have been what she saw and heard at Chiefswood that inspired her to write such romantic and soulful reflections of the Indian heart. However, it is also known that her parents encouraged her to write verse and ensured the presence of worthwhile books in their home.

A story is told of Alexander Graham Bell and Pauline's father, George Johnson, walking through woods and fields, and up and down slopes one day in July of 1876. They were stringing the two miles of stovewire that led from the telegraph office in Brantford to the Bell farmhouse. Bell, then 29 years of age, was already known for both his success as a teacher of deaf mutes and his ideas on the transmission of sounds.

Guests had assembled at the Bell farmhouse that day, curious to see the latest experiment. The telegrapher at the station in Brantford let out a whoop, "I can hear you splendidly, Professor!" Later words came in staccato gutturals and all that came through the receiver was something like,

Chiefswood was the home of Indian poet Pauline Johnson and at one time was the capital of Indian Canada. Surrounded by trees, this house overlooks the Grand River below Middleport.

"Sago gatchi ska na ka," with laughter in the background.[20] The telegrapher responded, "Are all you fellows drunk up there?" The answer from Bell, clear and loud was, "You've insulted Chief Johnson. He's been speaking in Mohawk."[21]

This may have been the unofficial first instance of long-distance talking on a telephone. The official instance between Brantford and nearby Paris, when two telephones operated satisfactorily on one circuit, is recorded on a plaque in Paris, dated August 29, 1877. The fourteen-year-old Pauline was in attendance at a supper celebration gathering for the occasion of the experiment, along with her mother and father.

Pauline's public appearances began in 1892. Taking after her grandfather, John Smoke Johnson and his colourful oratory, Pauline dressed for the stage in a fringed buckskin suit adorned with jewellery carved by Mohawk silversmiths and a scarlet blanket thrown around her shoulders. A wampum belt, a dagger and a necklace of the claws of the cinnamon bear and a single eagle plume completed the outfit.

Often Pauline was described as a lyric singer of nature and a balladist who played words like branches in the breeze. A writer of both prose and poetry, she had a remarkable memory and charming personality. Most notably she was a gifted elocutionist, reciting her enthralling poems as only she could interpret them to captivated audiences across Canada and the United States and Europe.

Her most famous work, initially recited in Toronto, *The Song My Paddle Sings,* brought her fame. Sold to *The Week* of Toronto for $1.00, this poem helped launch a series of recitations that continued for some nineteen years.

Her first book, *The White Wampum,* was published in England in the 1890's during the period of her most auspicious success. Following extensive periods of touring, Pauline would always return to Canada where she became known as the first Canadian woman, first Canadian Indian and first Canadian writer of international fame. Later she settled in Vancouver, British Columbia where she did her best writing, much of it developed from the legends of the Squamish Reserve.

However, Pauline was not in Vancouver long before she knew she was soon to die of tuberculosis. She passed away at the age of fifty-two on March 7, 1913. *Flint and Feather,* her best-known publication, appeared after her death.

When she died, journalist Ecclestone MacKay described the effect of her verse in *Canadian Magazine* in an article entitled "Pauline Johnson: A Remembrance": "First it brings a breath of the woods, warm and fragrant, a breath which clutches at the throat . . . the sound of swiftly-flowing water, the splash of a leaping trout, the dip of a paddle . . . And with all these lovely and familiar things it brings also something fainter, more remote, more primitive: the strain of an earlier, bolder, cruder race."[22]

During her lifetime, despite her acknowledged fame, the entire income earned from sale of her poems is reputed to have been only about $500. Today a large plaque, unveiled May 17, 1986 stands

Chocolates / Chocolats
Chocolate Manufacturers Since 1921   450 g

Box top of chocolates manufactured in Vancouver, B.C., to commemorate Pauline Johnson.

at Chiefswood Museum in honour of the famous Canadian poet.

Besides the memorials to her honour in Vancouver, people in British Columbia know of her through the well-known "Pauline Johnson" chocolates. Their popularity was described by a local person this way: as Ganong chocolates are in eastern Canada and Laura Secord chocolates are in central Canada, Pauline Johnson chocolates are in Western Canada. Today the Pauline Johnson chocolates are manufactured according to the traditional standards set by the founders in 1921.

> THE CAMPER
> by Emily Pauline Johnson (Tekahionwake)
>
> Night 'neath the northern skies, lone black, and grim;
> Naught but the starlight lies 'twixt heaven, and him.
> Of man no need has he, of God, no prayer;
> He and his Deity are brothers there.
> Above his bivouac the firs fling down
> Through branches gaunt and black, their needles brown.
> Afar some mountain streams, rockbound and fleet,
> Sing themselves through his dreams in cadence sweet.
> The pine trees whispering, the heron's cry,
> The plover's passing wing, his lullaby
> And blinking overhead the white stars keep
> Watch o'er his hemlock bed – his sinless sleep.

Peter Robertson, Inventor of the Robertson Screwnail

Peter Lymburner Robertson was born and raised not far from Caledonia in Seneca township, one of a family of six children born to John and Annie Robertson. His father would die in the Yukon in 1886, bitten by the Gold Fever, leaving Peter's mother to raise the family. Of the other children, John Junior went to Nevada, Will became a doctor in Toronto, Hutton taught school and later took up dentistry, Jessie married and Isa remained single at least until the time she left Seneca.

Peter, a mechanically minded person with an entrepreneurial bent, began his career as an agent or salesman. In 1907 he established the P.L. Robertson Manufacturing Company in Hamilton. A year later it was relocated to nearby Milton. This company is known to be the first firm in the world to produce the square recessed screw and the accompanying screw driver, patented in many countries throughout the world as the Robertson screw. The Ontario inventor used an ingenious process he had developed to punch square holes into cold metal, then developing the innovative screw for industrial markets. The Robertson screw is still used around the world today.

In the company's first two decades it steadily expanded operations and by 1930 when the last patent on the Robertson screw and the equipment used in its manufacture expired, the firm had already begun to diversify its products.

The very early years had been tough going. Peter's company had a difficult time breaking into the manufacturing field in opposition to some large companies already positioned in the market place. However, with his innovation and his perseverance and with support from the emerging Ford Company standing behind him, Robertson succeeded. At one time P.L. Robertson Manufacturing shipped a twenty-ton order of screws to England.

On November 8, 1986, the Milton Historical Society and the Ontario Heritage Foundation commemorated the location on Bronte Street where, from 1908 to 1951, Peter Lymburner Robertson invented the screw and screwdriver and went on to achieve international manufacturing recognition. Also the financial assistance from the Ontario Ministry of Citizenship and Culture and the Town of Milton led to a plaque being unveiled to indicate the location on Martin Street where Robertson lived as a life-long bachelor from 1916 until he died in 1951. Milton considers the Seneca township-born Peter Robertson to be one of its most considerate benefactors as well as an industrialist, inventor and author. In 1934 he wrote a remarkable book entitled *The Gold Standard* which won acclaim in many circles.

The Company is now operated as Robertson Whitehouse Company, one of the largest manufacturers in North America of light fasteners and the original Robertson screw.

An Area Knight: Sir Byron Edmond Walker

His name was Sir Byron Edmund Walker and the nobility honour was bestowed for distinction in the financial world. Born in Seneca township just on the outskirts of Caledonia on October 14, 1848, he was raised on a farm as one of nine children. His parents were Alfred E. Walker and Fanny Murton.

Walker's financial career began in 1868 with the Canadian Bank of Commerce. At the age of twelve he left school to work in his uncle's bank in Hamilton. Thirty years later he became President of the bank and retained this position until he died in Toronto on March 27, 1924, at the age of seventy-six.

While an authority on banking, he was also extensively interested in the humanities and in particular, in heritage. He wrote a history of Canadian banking and many pamphlets on related subjects. To this day his name is listed by the Champlain Society as its first president (1905-1925) and a founding member in 1905. He was also one of the founders and prime backers of both the Toronto Art Gallery and the Royal Ontario Museum. The list of public involvement goes on and on, from being a board member of the Toronto Conservatory of Music in 1901, being an Honorary President of the Mendelssohn Choir from 1900-1924, to his role as the President of the Royal Canadian Institute in 1898. As well, he had the distinction of being the financial mentor to the Right Honourable Sir Robert Borden.

Sir Edmund helped found the *Round Table Quarterly* to promote discussion of imperial issues. He was knighted by King George V in 1910. Joseph Schull's *Ontario Since 1867* quotes Sir Edmund Walker as President of the Bank of Commerce in 1913. At that time roads were built for horse and buggy use and automobiles were slowly winning grudging acceptance. Sir Edmund, a true financier, said, "If we had good roads in Ontario people would come in increasing numbers from the United States . . . there is no question of an increase in the number of motors so great that we would soon be issuing 20,000 licenses for cars . . .say at $25 each . . . $500,000 – quite a contribution."[23] One of those bad roads he spoke of would have been the plank road from Hamilton to Port Dover which by that time had been covered with six feet of gravel.

At the same time, he opposed the policy of free trade with the U.S. as announced by the Sir Wilfrid Laurier government because he felt it would weaken ties with Great Britain. History tells us that this surge of Imperialism expressed in Canada led to the defeat of the trade agreement and ultimately the government.

Sir Byron Edmund Walker, not generally recognized as a Caledonia boy, was a leading citizen of Canada in his day. His foresight and supportive initiatives were in many instances responsible for some exceptional institutions that are still a prominent part of our society today.

Married to Mary Alexander, daughter of Alexander Alexander of Hamilton, he had four sons and three daughters. Sir Edmund Walker's distinguished career ended with his death in 1924.

William Doyle

A walking encyclopedia was how one person described William (Billy) Doyle. At age ninety-one in 1956 he had recollections that went back to the 1870's when he was a young boy. He was named for his father, William Doyle, who had been the constable in Caledonia from 1871 to 1878. Billy remembered the flour mill in Caledonia and Chris Young's Seneca House in Seneca Village. He also recalled that

in the post-navigation days, there were two shipping wharves and a warehouse just east of the bridge on the north bank, as well as a wharf west of the bridge and another warehouse and wharf on the south side of the river.

Billy Doyle was in the McKinnon Woollen Mill in 1881 when it burned. He claimed then and repeated it in 1956 that it was burned on purpose. Mr. McKinnon had died in 1879 and he claimed the mill was being operated by people he regarded as crooks.

Billy Doyle.

In 1885 Doyle read of his own death in *The Sachem*. At the time he was working on bridge construction in Northern Ontario where there had been an accident. Fortunately he had not been involved.

Billy Doyle died February 16, 1963 in his ninety-ninth year in Pomino, New York. His daughter, Margaret O'Rourke, lives in Caledonia, but all other members of his family live in New York State.

Bruce E. French

Bruce French's keen interest in the community led him to compile the first detailed history of Caledonia in 1927, in time for the Diamond Anniversary of Confederation. He had taught school in Cayuga before buying R. E. Walker's hardware business which occupied the building still standing on the southeast corner of Caithness St. and Argyle. He remained in business from 1905 until 1942 when the store was sold to H.S. Merrell. A prominent citizen of Caledonia during his years in business, Bruce French is said to have been a "real gentleman". There weren't many organizations and community events where he wasn't listed as an officer or volunteer.

The 1927 history, entitled A *Short Historical Sketch of Caledonia* was written when he was Reeve of Caledonia. The history's intricate detail spanned the years from 1784 through to 1927, taking column after column of space in *The Grand River Sachem*'s special souvenir edition. Authors of histories since then have referred to these columns, truly a remarkable contribution to the maintenance of our sense of history. Unfortunately, ill-health prevented his completion of a history on St. Paul's Anglican Church. Bruce French passed away, leaving his wife Flo, the former Florence Lawson.

Bruce French, recorder of Caledonia's history at time of Diamond Jubilee celebrations in 1927.

She remained in their home at the northeast corner of Edinburgh Square until her death in the early 1980's at ninety-six years of age. She too, retained memories of the community and often was called upon to relay them for historical purposes. The family home stands on part of the property where Scott's Iron Foundry stood from 1850-1880.

Following the death of their daughter Helen, in November 1989, the estate opened the home to the public by selling the family belongings in a public auction. The antique furniture, books and fine china attracted dealers and citizens from miles around. One piece of furniture was identified as to having come from the John Builder Furniture Factory, a business in Caledonia in 1866. Today the home is in private hands, the former belongings and treasures from Caledonia scattered across Ontario and perhaps beyond.

Mrs. Fleming's "English Pink Ointment"

Etta Fleming did not need advertising to sell her sought-after product. It was more popular than the best on the market. Patented in 1931, Etta manufactured her home recipe for a healing salve under the label "English Pink Ointment" for almost thirty years. An old family recipe passed down for generations in

The well-known English Pink Ointment! A much sought-after remedy for burns, cuts and scalds.

England on her husband Wesley Fleming's side, Etta was responsible for its popularity in Canada's Caledonia area.

She ordered the ingredients, the small one-ounce tins and the labels from Boose's Drug Store. Stan Parke, a former druggist, remembers that customer's claimed that Mrs. Fleming's ointment was faster-acting than Mecca or the Zambuck salve. Once she had made the English Pink Ointment and carefully packaged it, Etta would sell her product back to the drugstore for availability to customers.

Etta Fleming, the creator of the English Pink Ointment, shown with her husband Wesley.

Frankie Szabo, her son-in-law, said she didn't make a great deal of money on "E.P.O.", as it became known, but kept making it to accommodate the customers who wouldn't be without it. In the 1940's the ointment sold for 50 cents at the drugstore. "Once she got older, she had me stir and mix it for her," Frank said. Etta's recipe has been passed down and is recorded as follows: 2 – 1 lb. tins of white petroleum (vaseline); 2 1/2 oz. olive oil; 2 tsp. oil of thyme; 4 oz. calamine; 2 oz. of mercury red oxide granulated. Mix and stir.

It was the drawing power of the recipe that gave the ointment the healing quality for sores, cuts, burns and scratches. For boils, it was the answer to drawing out the core. The value of the ointment went beyond people to become a local remedy for horses and other domestic animals.

Etta, her husband Wes, and their two daughters lived in the Seneca

Village area at 696 Caithness St. East during the 1930's and 40's. Later they would move to the south side of the river. At one time, they lived in the Richardson (Haldimand House) apartment complex. Etta died in August, 1977 at a Hagersville nursing home where she and her husband had lived for sometime. She was eighty-eight years old.

He Walked Alone

His name was Lloyd A. Culp, but the community knew him as "Tuffy". His sense of priorities were different from those of the average person, but then as one might put it, who are we to say he was wrong and we were right. His free spirit allowed him to enjoy life as he lived it. He was one of four children born to Bill and Lizzie Culp, the one who decided to live life differently.

Tuffy lived a good mile or more away from the centre of town, but would be seen daily with at least two suits of clothing, winter or summer, usually pulling his wagon. If the business people didn't see him for a day or two, there would be concerns about his whereabouts and well-being.

Earl Gillespie's residence was about halfway between Tuffy's home and the downtown area. Tuffy would call in almost every day to get a drink of water. Eventually the Gillespies put a glass by the outside tap ready for his visit just in case he called when no one was home.

Tuffy was known to be a gentleman. He was always polite unless provoked. He usually played along with any teasing, but if it got out of hand he would be upset. He was fair, honest and appreciative of any kindness. He knew who his friends were and would call on them for help when needed. One such friend remembered Tuffy bor-

A familiar figure on the streets of Caledonia, Lloyd "Tuffy" Culp died in 1979.

rowing $2.00 until his cheque came in. When he couldn't pay it back at the time promised, he went to his lender to tell him he just didn't have the money. It was a month before it was paid back, but Tuffy hadn't forgotten. This isn't an unusual story, it's one that is told often by different people.

Fair time was looked forward to by Tuffy. That was one of the many times during the year he would enter the Sachem office without a hello and walk straight back to his friend Harrison Martindale in the print shop, to ask for the list of Fair dates. He wanted to be ready for his job with the Marshall concession where he peeled potatoes. Tuffy travelled with the Marshalls from fair to fair, including the one at Caledonia. In his younger days, at haying time he would work for some farmers in the area, and according to those who hired him, did a good days work.

The doctors would also look after Tuffy. He was confined to hospital on more than one occasion. The last time was just before his death when a terminal illness kept him hospitalized for some time. Lloyd died November 22, 1979.

Harrison's poetic prose led him to write an obituary about his friend to mark the end of an era. Familiar individuals such as Tuffy were to be no longer part of a town's makeup. Harrison writes, "'Tuffy' as he was affectionately called by all who knew him was a familiar figure in our community. He was known to almost everyone in Caledonia, especially the children in our town."

"Lloyd never owned an automobile of any kind but his wagon was just as important and dear to him as if it had been a shiny limousine. It was the finest wagon in town, complete with license plates, rubber tired wheels and safety reflector mirrors. His wagon was a part of his life and it followed him wherever he went, and it was often seen parked on the sidewalk on our main street.

"No doubt there were often times when Lloyd felt rejected by our modern day society and his loneliness was always hidden from the eyes of the busy passerby.

"We knew Lloyd Culp to be an honest man; a man who knew no violence and profanity which held no place in his conversation.

"Our old friend will not be remembered for his monetary or material possessions, but rather he will be remembered as a familiar figure who walked alone, without malice or bitterness, and demanding so very little from the world in which he lived."[24]

The Six Nations Artist

Known as "The Six Nations Artist", Chief Beaver travelled the Grand River from Caledonia to Brantford in the 1890's, painting houses and business buildings for a living. During his life span from 1846 to 1925 he lived at Beaver's Corners near Ohsweken on the Six Nations Reserve. A gifted man of many talents, he was known as a carpenter, a wood-carver,

The Six Nations artist Chief Beaver took his juggling show from town to town. Many of his paintings are of buildings or scenery located in the small towns he visited while performing.

a juggler and a showman, as well as a painter.

On stage, he was "Uncle Beaver" as he travelled across Canada and the United States with road shows, carnivals and medicine men. Today some homes on the Reserve still retain samples of his woodworking and fine carpentry skills.

Jim Beaver and his wife, Lydia (Bay) from a Mohawk Reserve in Quebec, raised three sons and four daughters. Granddaughter Alta Doxtador remembered being impressed by a concert her grandfather put on in Christ Church at Beaver's Corners and the canvas backdrops he painted for the occasion. She also remembered seeing him seated in front of his easel. Because he couldn't read or write, he once asked her to write TITANIC on a paper for his painting of a ship.

Mrs. Emily Ames, the daughter of H.B. Sawle, one-time publisher of *The Sachem*, remembered Chief Beaver asking to paint the Sachem building for a sum of money. She and her sister (Mrs. Harrison Arrell) were very young when they posed with the rest of the family in front of the building in 1892. That particular Chief Beaver painting hung in the *Sachem* office until the early

The Sachem newspaper building was painted by Chief Beaver in 1892. The original was restored and now belongs to Edinburgh Square Heritage and Cultural Centre.

This original Chief Beaver painting of Niagara Falls is owned by the Iroquois Indian Museum in New York.

1980's when it was later donated by the Martindale family to Edinburgh Square Heritage and Cultural Centre where it hangs today. Because of its historic significance to the area, full government funding by the Ministry of Citizenship and Culture enabled the restoration of this important piece of art to take place.

Today Chief Beaver's paintings are valuable. Numerous residents were offered large sums of money for their Beaver originals some fifteen years ago. Edinburgh Square Heritage and Cultural Centre has two Chief Beaver originals; the "Three Sister Mountains" and the "Sachem Newspaper Office". The Iroquois Indian Museum in New York State also has a number of Chief Beaver originals as does the Woodland Cultural Educational Centre in Brantford.

Pine kitchen cupboard crafted by Jim Beaver, c. 1890.

Landmarks

Edinburgh Square

Edinburgh Square has held a certain aura for Caledonians throughout the existence of the town. One always knew that when noise was heard in the Square, something of importance was happening.

For many years Edinburgh Square was one of five planned squares. The first Horticultural Society, organized in 1910, planted many trees on Edinburgh Square some of which are still standing around the Cenotaph. Peonies once lined the avenue leading to the front step of the Town Hall. Ornamental shrubs and plants were also placed on the other four squares. Prior to the building of the Town Hall in 1857, Edinburgh Square was known as Market Square. Here farmer's produce and meats were sold by vendors.

In 1864 a private school, housed in a frame building, began operation on the Square where the lawnbowling clubhouse is located today. This school was later moved to make room for weighscales and the village animal pound. Lawnbowling began in H.B. Sawle's backyard on Sutherland Street. By the turn of the century a green was being laid out at its present location in Edinburgh Square.

One block west of Argyle, paralleling the east side of Edinburgh Square, was Glasgow Square. The other three village squares were on the south side: St. Andrews Square at Stirling and Argyle Streets, then known as Dumfries; Greenock Square at Perth and Selkirk and Paisley Square on Peebles Street just north west of Kinross.

A Drill Hall was built by the Caledonia Rifles on Glasgow Square in 1866. It opened November 22, 1867 as Glasgow Hall. A few years later it was moved to Edinburgh Square's northeast corner as the drill hall for the Caledonia Agriculture and Art Society's annual Caledonia Fair to ex-

Photographed from the north end of the bridge in 1902, the Caledonia Band, Firemen and residents celebrate the Boer War's Relief of Ladysmith as they parade along Argyle Street to the southside of town. At the left of the picture C. Donaghy and Sam Overend are in the buggy with the white horse, T. Smith is with the drum and T. Emerson has the cornet. Also in the picture are J. Murphy, H. Tregaskis, S. Avery and Phil Young.

hibit grain and produce. From 1872 to 1876 the annual Fair was held on Edinburgh Square. The Drill Hall was then moved to the present fairgrounds where it remained until 1924 when the arena was built. Today the Square is used at Fair time to park cars.

Little league baseball is still played at the Square. However, at one time Edinburgh Square's baseball diamond was the only one in town and huge crowds came to watch hardball at its best. Over the years tennis, lacrosse, boxing, skating on an outdoor rink and football have been played on the Square. Rodeos and a popular annual circus also were held on this popular location. Until 1950 Garden Parties were held there during the July 1 celebrations. Those holiday events usually included an all-day baseball tournament which continued until Garden Parties were relocated to the Band Shell in Kinsmen Park on the west side of town.

The Square was also the centre for political rallies. Many political platforms were aired there to the large crowds who gathered to hear and discuss issues of the day. In the days before television this was the only chance for voters to see and hear the Party Leaders and politicians of that era.

Today Edinburgh Square's baseball diamond is one of five busy diamonds in Caledonia. The lawnbowling green there remains the only one in town. The Cenotaph each year draws large crowds for the November 11 Remembrance Day services. The number of cars parked on the square the first weekend in October indicates how large the crowd is for the annual Caledonia Fair held just east of the square on the fairgrounds. Some years an outdoor ice rink during the winter months attracts hockey and skating enthusiasts from all parts of the community. Edinburgh Square is indeed a year-round centre of activity in Caledonia.

The Old Town Hall

The Town Hall opened for its first council meeting on January 18, 1858. The architect was John Turner, a well-respected businessman and citizen of Brantford who had come to Canada from Great Britain in 1839. Turner was responsible for the design and construction of many fine public and commercial buildings erected across Southwestern Ontario between 1850 and 1886. Some of his building achievements include court houses in St. Thomas and Simcoe and churches, such as St. Basil's Roman Catholic and Park Baptist in Brantford. John Turner died in Brantford in 1887.

The Town Hall soon became the centre of the community. The base-

Edinburgh Square in 1910 when tennis was played and where lawn bowlers in their whites are found today. A bandstand stood in those days, where the war memorial, erected in 1922, stands today. (A private postcard, McGregor & Co.)

Edinburgh Square Heritage and Cultural Centre (formerly the old Town Hall) stands as a monument to Caledonia's past.

ment housed the jail and a meat market. Stalls were set up for butchers to carry on business inside the "Caledonia Market House", advertised to be open everyday except Sunday. Until 1955 the main floor held the apartment quarters for the town's constable. The Constable's wife was expected to serve meals to the prisoners, who were usually locked up for drunkenness.

The town's character of the 1930's was a frequent guest in the jail. The story is told of this fellow who as a young lad knew the Bible well and wanted to be a preacher. He didn't fulfill his ambition, but instead cleaned septic tanks for a living and became a habitual drinker. One day during a spring flood, he was seen sitting in front of his house on the river bank just west of the bridge with a bottle of spirits in hand while the Grand River rose around him, singing in a loud voice "Rescue the Perishing". He was rushed off to jail where, it was said, he always enjoyed his stay.

The top floor of the Town Hall was used by Council for meetings and as a hall for social events. Happenings as diverse as Chautauqua Shows, concerts, wrestling matches, court hearings, short courses and W.I. meetings were once held here. Boy Scouts and Girl Guides had weekly nights for group meetings. A library was housed on the upper floor as well. In 1917, the year women first got their vote, a polling station was located there. Some senior Caledonians still remember that landmark day for Canada.

After 1955 Council meetings were held on the main floor. Other than a place for the Public Utilities administration, Red Cross storage and a lawn bowling clubhouse, the Town Hall became relatively inactive. It stood almost vacant after Regional Government took over municipal affairs in 1974. At that time all administrative activities and Council Meetings were moved to an administration building in Cayuga.

Never had there been such an eruption of public outcry as in 1974

The jail cell in the old Town Hall (Edinburgh Square Heritage and Cultural Centre).

when it was suggested the Town Hall should be torn down to make room for parking facilities. Although the Public Utilities office had remained in the building, essentially it was unused and needed many repairs. However, as a consequence of the public uproar over the suggestion of demolition, the Town Hall was saved. On January 25, 1982 it was designated as a Heritage building, on its way to becoming a museum, ensuring its place of pride and usefulness in the community.

The Town Hall's exterior was given a complete facelift, including wheelchair accessibility. During a colourful ceremony in September of 1983 a replica of the original cupola was lifted to its rooftop. A fundraising committee was established the following year to begin the long arduous trek toward renovating the inside in preparation for its becoming a museum. It would

The replica of the Town Hall's cupola was carefully placed during a ceremony in 1982.

not be until the spring of 1988 that the old Town Hall was finally reopened, this time as the Edinburgh Square Heritage and Cultural Centre.

Today the main floor holds a display room for the historical artifacts of years gone by, along with office and washroom facilities. The modern staircase has been relocated to make the basement and the third floor area easily accessible. The meat market found years ago on the basement level is now a work area for preparing artifacts for display. As well, a gift shop has been included in this area. The "public lock-up" jail cell remains as a remembrance of the Town Hall's beginning. Even the monstrous safe has been kept for storage of valuables.

The third floor is once again a meeting room for community events. A small kitchenette and the Gillespie Clark Library Resource Centre is

filled with books and documents containing town history. Here the
Grand River Sachem newspaper files from 1856 to the present day can be
researched in the library. A piano has been donated by The Music Teach-
ers Association and placed in the meeting room for small concerts and
recitals. Currently the Edinburgh Square Heritage and Cultural Centre
is administered by The Town of Haldimand, a Board of Directors, a Cu-
rator, Barbara Lang Walker and an enthusiastic group of volunteers. It is
a proud symbol of the achievement of a heritage-minded community.

The Landmark – The Caledonia Bridge

More than sixty years old, this symbol of Caledonia was said in 1927 to
be the first reinforced concrete arch bridge ever built. Today it is recognized as the only nine-span bridge of its kind in Canada.

Built by the Department of Public Highways of Ontario, its contractor

Caledonia's famous nine-span bridge, the only one of its kind in Canada.

was the Randolph Macdonald Company Limited of Toronto and the designing engineer was A.B. Crealock from the Ontario Department of Public Highways. Work was completed in just one hundred and forty working days from June 7th to November 19th, 1927, a major feat of the time.

The bridge is 700 feet long with eight concrete piers and two concrete abutments. Each of the nine spans is 72 feet 7 inches (21.12 metres) long. The width is about 42 feet (12.5 metres) with sidewalk and hand-railing on each side. Its strength is attributed to the bow-string-type trusses. The bow strings are of reinforced concrete with square columns which support the spans. The foundations for the piers were excavated to solid ground rock and the concrete poured on this foundation.

A gala two-day affair was held to open the newly completed bridge. The celebration included a dance sponsored by the Caledonia Fire Brigade on that very mild Friday November evening. On Saturday, people from the district gathered on the bridge in the afternoon to hear provincial government officials pay tribute. The bridge was declared officially open at 3:00 p.m. when a pair of gold scissors used by T.J. Mahony, M.L.A. for South Wentworth, severed the wide white satin ribbon at the north end. A procession led by the Caledonia Citizen Band was the first to cross the new bridge and the first car to cross carried the wife of the contractor.

The crowd then adjourned to the Opera House to hear a program of laudatory speeches including one by B.E. French, Reeve of Caledonia, who declared the new bridge second to none in the province. Members of County Council, Town Council and other dignitaries moved on to the Union Hotel to conclude the festivities.

Just after the crowd had dispersed from the bridge location, a runaway horse couldn't resist the attraction. The Sachem reported that R.J. Thompson was driving down Argyle Street in a democrat, sitting on a cream can and holding a gasoline engine, when the breeching strap on the harness broke. His horse panicked and couldn't be stopped until it reached the other side of the bridge. No one was hurt, but spectators said the first runaway over the new bridge was a real John Gilpin ride.[25]

During the summer of 1984 extensive repairs were made to the bridge to further strengthen the structure for today's heavy traffic. Motorists continue to use the bridge despite the construction a year before of a bypass around Caledonia to lessen traffic passing through the town.

The old iron bridge over the Grand at Caledonia, built in 1875.

Former Bridges

There had been two permanent bridges built before the present bridge. The first was a sixty feet wide wooden structure, reinforced with steel plates. It had six spans, one of which was a swing section. Built in 1842, it lasted for only nineteen years until jams of ice floes and floating logs destroyed it during the spring thaw of 1861.

Temporary bridges were built between 1861 and 1875. Although the Halidmand Navigation Company still held navigation rights on the river there was little river traffic to warrant building a swing section on a new bridge. For a sum of $400 they agreed to dispense with this requirement. Consequently a new solid iron structure was built at a cost of $22,500 with a Toll House going up to pay the debt.

This 1875 bridge had six spans of 105 feet (32 metres) each supported by a cast iron bow-string truss manufactured at the Scott Foundry of Caledonia. It was built with a wood floor, a wooden wall on either side for protection and a six foot wooden sidewalk along the west side. A swing iron gate at the north end prevented drivers from passing through without paying the toll.

This bridge withstood the raging Grand River, in particular the spring floods, for fifty years. There are people who still remember the disaster

When the Iron Bridge went down in 1925, this truck went with it.

that occurred at 3 p.m. on Monday, August 24, 1925. A large truck loaded with stone, driving from the south end reached the middle span only to have the span collapse behind it. The driver felt the rear of the truck tilt downward and instantaneously the air was filled with flying timber and iron. Truck, driver and span dropped into the river some 30 feet (9 metres) below. Somehow the vehicle remained upright when it struck the river bed. Miraculously, the driver was unhurt. He immediately jumped out of the truck to rescue a boy who had disappeared with the fallen sidewalk. Twenty children bathing in the shallow water under the fourth pier were uninjured.

When the span collapsed, it was described as "the bang that woke the town". Women at their clotheslines on that Monday afternoon wondered what had happened. Others busy with their summer canning were upset at having the gas go off. The gas main had been broken as a result of the collapse and there was some fear of an explosion. However, their concerns were unfounded and repairs took place very quickly. The span also was reconstructed and the bridge was reopened to traffic on September 30th, 1925.

Negotiations immediately took place between the Provincial Government and County Council for the construction of a new bridge. The old one was demolished by the contractor to make room for the new bridge. During construction, in the summer of 1927, a temporary bridge was erected to the west of the construction site to accommodate the welcoming home of the Old Boys and Girls of Caledonia.

The Bridge Without A Reason

There is a small steel bridge in the Caledonia vicinity that will not wear out from use. This bridge is known today as Seneca Bridge, but was known previously as Black Creek Bridge. Located on the eastern outskirts of Caledonia in Seneca Park, it appears to be a bridge built without a reason, but the historic plaque placed there in 1989 stamps it as a heritage site.

Contractor Melvin Runchey constructed the steel rod structure for $1,400 in 1913. The Hamilton Bridge Works was paid $1,000 for steel structure material, J.H. Creighton was paid almost $100 for providing planking and the Caledonia Milling Company $114.50 for cement and lumber. Contractor Runchey offered his services for $100 per month and was paid $200.

Seneca Park's historic Seneca Bridge, today used only as a pedestrian walkway.

Originally the old river road needed a bridge to cross Black Creek until 1950. The building of the new No. 54 highway led to the route of the creek being diverted to flow into the river west of the bridge. The bridge lost its purpose. If there is a reason for Seneca Bridge today, it is as a reminder of those days when travelling and the pace of life were not as hectic.

The Old Mill

The Old Mill is the only mill left. Today it stands to remind us of the early milling days in Caledonia. Its historic importance was recognized by the Local Architectural Conservation Advisory Committee (LACAC) in 1989 when it was declared a Heritage building. The Mill was built by James Little in the 1850's to process wheat into flour. Considered to be the best example of an operational mill left on the river, it is a monument to the community's beginning.

The Golden Horseshoe Antique Society was assigned by the Town of Haldimand to manage the restoration of the Old Mill. The Society has solicited co-operation from the York-Grand River Historical Society for this project. Although the inside remains untouched, the outside has been refurbished with paint and attractive lighting and the building has been wired for security.

Plans for restoration are extensive. The committee hopes to divert water from the Grand River into the millrace to re-activate the original power turbines which are still intact and operable. Some of the milling

View from the north bank of the Grand River just west of the bridge, with the Old Mill on the right.

machinery had been removed by the Grand River Conservation Authority in 1980 to refurbish Apps Mill near Paris. However, the restoration committee, spearheaded by enthusiasts Fred Thompson and Alf Peart, has acquired most of the missing machinery from various sources.

Authentic Caledonia Milling Co. "Peerless" flour bags and "Peerless" flour barrel top labels were left in the Old Mill from the days of operation. The Restoration Committee presents laminated originals to those whose generous donations enable the restoration work to move forward. The Old Mill, situated just east of the Caledonia bridge, provides background scenery for photographers wanting to capture the heritage essence of Caledonia's beginning.

Built To Take Tolls

The Toll House stands today as a reminder that once upon a time a toll was paid every time one crossed the Caledonia bridge. This substantial brick building, located in the downtown area at the north end of the bridge, was built in 1875 at the same time as the bridge. Constructed spe-

The Toll House built in 1875 and still standing at the northern end of the bridge.

cifically as a residence for the Toll Keeper, it was used for this purpose until the late 1800's. The County owned both the Bridge and Toll House and sold the right to collect tolls. The person who had the highest tender lived in the Toll House and, of course, made sure no-one passed over without paying.

In 1856 a warning was published that, "the travelling public may as well observe that nothing is to be gained by taking to the ice and avoiding the toll for the Bridge, spanning the River at this place. On Monday last a span of horses crossing the ice, broke through and were rescued with much difficulty. On arriving at the east side of the stream, the gate-keeper demanded the toll and we believe got it. Teamsters will please make a note and govern themselves accordingly."[26]

Before tolls were abolished, the rate for a team of horses was 25 cents while a single horse return was 15 cents. Tolls were also charged for carriages, cows and oxen, sheep and swine. The Toll Keeper would shut the swing iron gate at the north end of the bridge at night to prevent drivers from passing through without paying the fee. However, before the new bridge was built in 1864, the Toll Keeper protested the poor condition of the old wooden bridge by refusing to make collections.

A small boy by the name of James Tutton died November 15, 1850 as a result of drinking whiskey he found in the former Toll House. He was only four years old. This may or may not explain a story that the present century-plus old house is haunted. Despite these tales, the Toll House has been privately owned for many years, and is still standing by the bridge along the banks of the Grand.

The Oldest Surviving Business: Caledonia's Newspaper

The oldest business in Caledonia is *The Grand River Sachem*. It began in 1856 when Thomas Messenger came from Cayuga to start a newspaper in Caledonia. At the time he was publishing the *Cayuga Sachem* and was ready to expand his publishing interests. Until November of that same year, Messenger published under the banner, *The Caledonia Advertiser*. He then sold the *Cayuga Sachem* and claimed the Sachem name for his Caledonia paper.

As a publisher he had strong convictions and did not hesitate to print them publicly. "He is a freeman whom the truth makes free and all are slaves besides" was added to the banner in 1858. That quotation and the Sachem name remains with the Caledonia newspaper to this day.

In many ways *Sachem* was an appropriate name for its founder who also took on "Sachem" as a nickname. A Sachem was a Chief among the Indian tribes whose duties included carrying the news home from meetings with other clans and tribes. A Sachem was known to be one with wisdom who was carefully selected for the position by the clan mother.

Some early writers at the *Sachem* used the experience developed in Caledonia as the foundation for building their careers. Brick Pomeroy went on to become a famous col-

Thomas Messenger, founder of the *Grand River Sachem*, 1856.

umnist with the *New York World* and wrote a popular column titled "Words of Wisdom". His motto was "fearless and incorruptible". James Fedro learned to set type so fast at the *Sachem* that he was believed to be the fastest hand compositor in America. He went to the United States to expand his opportunities, but later came back to Caledonia and ended his days in the *Sachem* office in the 1920's.

Thomas Messenger owned the newspaper until his passing in 1875. Previous to his death, a man by the name of W.T. Sawle had arrived from Buffalo via the Grand River. He had heard there was an opening at the *Grand River Sachem*. This would lead to the Sawle line of ownership. Henry B. Sawle, W.T.'s

Harrison Martindale, associated with the *Grand River Sachem* for 54 years.

brother, bought the newspaper in 1882 and when he died in 1923, his second wife Mary Florence took over. She was known to be one of the

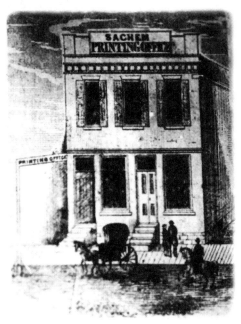

The *Grand River Sachem* building 1856–1865 on Caithness Street.

first women editors and publishers in Canada.[27]

In 1927 the young Harrison Martindale, began working for Mrs. Sawle. The Martindale line of ownership began when he and his brother Arrell purchased the *Sachem* in 1945. Harrison and his son Chester co-published from 1972 until Chester's untimely death in 1980. His wife Barbara took over his co-publishing duties. Harrison retired in 1981, but remained on the masthead as Publisher Emeritus up until his death early in 1995.

In May of 1982 the *Sachem* entered a new era. It became the sister paper to five other newspapers owned by Otter Publishing of Tillsonburg. Another transition took place when Otter Publishing was sold in 1987 to the Newfoundland Capital Corporation (N.C.C.), owners also of the Robinson Blackmore Group of thirteen papers in Newfoundland. Corporate owner of varied enterprises, the N.C.C. was on its way to ownership of fifteen papers in Ontario from Wingham to Delhi to Port Colborne.

The *Sachem* office is still located in the building erected by Messenger in 1865 to house his new newspaper. The first *Sachem* building was

Caledonia's *Grand River Sachem* newspaper has been doing business in this building since 1865.

on Caithness Street West on the north side. Until 1985 the newspaper and job printing were one. Today the *Sachem* printing is owned by Pressman's Printing of Caledonia, who also own the building. Since 1992 the newspaper has been independently owned by a group of shareholders in the community. Barbara Martindale returned as publisher in 1993.

Today the *Grand River Sachem* is not the only newspaper covering the community's news. The twenty-year-old *Regional News This Week* also has an office in town and distributes its newspapers to residents on a weekly basis.

Foundries and Factories

Caledonia's early history includes the Caledonia Foundry and Iron Works, better known as the Scott Foundry. Its huge stack was dominant from 1854 to 1881. The immense building extended from Edinburgh Square east, covering the property where today three houses stand, across from the fairgrounds. A stove once manufactured at the Scott Foundry is among the artifacts exhibited at Edinburgh Square Heritage and Cultural Centre.

In its early days, with John Scott as owner, the foundry manufactured all kinds of mill gearings and machinery in general. Later, its advertising featured a complete assortment of ploughs, harrow cultivators, horse rakes, threshing machines, stoves and other major products as available. These advertisements were distributed across Canada and the United States.

In 1862 a twenty-five horsepower engine was sent to Oil Springs, USA along with two, 1,700 pound each, box stoves designed for steaming purposes. At that same time the company was manufacturing a circular mill to be shipped to Thunder Bay, Michigan, the twelfth circular mill shipped out over a short period of time. Messrs. Scott and Company were congratulated in the newspaper for not only competing with American foundries, but surpassing them in the manufacture of circular mills.

While mills and foundries were part of many small towns getting their start in those years, the Caledonia Foundry and Iron Works seemed to excel. In addition to building an export business, the foundry looked to its local market and were responsible for the iron work on the 1875 Caledonia bridge.

During the same period, chair and furniture factories were important businesses in many beginning villages. Caledonia was no exception. The furniture factory owned by John Builder was in Caledonia, while the chair factory operated in the village of Seneca.

Caledonia as it appeared from the east in the 1860's, as represented in the *Canadian Illustrated News*, Hamilton, 1868. The Scott Foundry stack and the Town Hall are quite noticeable.

A March 1987 *City and Country Home* magazine article stipulated that rod-back dining chairs produced about 1850 in Caledonia area were still in existence as family heirlooms. Today, there are homes in Caledonia still possessing household furniture and chairs from that era.

Caledonia's Gypsum History

"It took five tons of Caledonia's Alabastine tinted pink to spray Yonge Street in Toronto for the Easter Parade. And after the parade it took Toronto firemen no time at all to wash it down the sewers." [28]

That bit of information is not generally known by Caledonia residents who have taken the chief industry of the town for granted since its beginning in 1905. But Earl Gillespie remembered that and much more. He was an integral part of the plant from 1937 to 1982 in research, development, management and technical areas.

According to the late Gillespie, the Grand's old river bed has everything to do with the discovery of gypsum deposits. Even the Hagersville's Canadian Gypsum Company mines, some ten miles away, are considered a coincidental result of the Grand River Valley's dried up sea beds.

The story of the "plaister beds" or gypsum goes back to 1822 when

William Holmes made the discovery on the banks of the Grand River, about a mile below the town of Paris, Ontario. A plant was established at Paris in 1896, and not long after, leases were taken out on gypsum deposits below York in Haldimand. This led, shortly thereafter, to the opening of the mine at Caledonia when gypsum was located there in 1905 while men were drilling for gas.

The gypsum rock was loaded into a one-ton car, hauled to the surface by a horse and dumped into a storage bin. It was then moved by wagon and donkey along a donkey track to the train, destined for Paris for processing. That first mine provided employment for many Caledonians over its more than fifty year span. Located just north of the plant and under No. 6 highway, the mine is no longer in use.

The second mine is a little more than a mile to the west of the first. The third location, now also being mined, is east of the highway. This mine may eventually extend much further to the east perhaps as far as the village of York.

Earl Gillespie remembered when it took a month to train the horses and donkeys that pulled the cars along eleven miles of track in the No. 1 mine. "Donkeys were used instead of horses because they would drop their heads to refrain from hitting the roof of the mine," he said. It was in the 1940's that the four-wheeled diesel-electric buggy came to Caledonia to replace the animals. It was Earl's responsibility to sell the twenty horses who had become friends of the workers, but were no longer needed.

The Ontario Gypsum Company operation at Caledonia in the 1950's, now Domtar.

A conference banquet in the gypsum mine in the 1930's.

He also remembered hearing about banquets being held in the mine during the very early years for some sixty people. Here the company would often host dealers to promote products. "They must have been rather cool affairs", he said, "the temperature in the mine remains at 55 degrees, winter or summer."

In the beginning, gypsum rock was ground to a fine powder and used as a carrier. The original Tom Morrison family who came to Caledonia from Scotland as stone dressers were skilled in using a hammer and chisel. "It is a real art in dressing stones that made the powder," said Earl.

At one time, a by-product known as Alatint was sold on the market as a potato bug killer, in a pink or green colour. One year it turned out to be grey. There were numerous complaints from customers who claimed the grey powder didn't do the job nearly as well. Earl told this story with a smile. He also remembered a Milton mushroom farmer bartering his truck load of mushrooms for a truck load of gypsum, a valuable fertilizer.

"Many don't realize that the Caledonia Plant was responsible for setting up other plants in Canada and in other countries," said Earl. For instance the Montreal East plant was built under Caledonia management to ship the Caledonia products to Scotland and England. The Caledonia

Plant also built sites at Rochester in Kent, England and in Sheildhall at Glasgow, Scotland. Caledonia's interest in both plants were later sold out to British Gypsum. Both are now owned by Westroc, a competitor of Domtar.

There were some one hundred and twenty-five employees in 1937 when Earl first joined the company, mainly residents of the town. But during World War II, people had to be brought in from other parts of the country. As Earl recalled, many came from Westinghouse and Stelco who were on strike at the time.

The war had a big effect on the Caledonia plant when wartime industries were needed. Hundreds of wartime houses were built very quickly around Hamilton and area with the new wallboard being produced at the Gypsum plant. Caledonia was the first to manufacture wallboard. Since 1916 it has been the chief product and today remains the primary product of the gypsum produced by Domtar Gypsum.

Another wartime effort included working with Fleet Aircraft to develop a formula of a mixture of Lumnite Cement and Plaster of Paris to produce the molds for the fenders of the Fleet aircraft. As well, the floors of all the arsenals used in Canada during the war came from the Caledonia plant. In addition, the Caledonia plant was one of the first manufacturers of Rock Wool when they used slag from Stelco in the production of insulation.

One of the three biggest companies in North America, Domtar Gypsum, as the company is now known, has been very aggressive in the last few years with takeovers in the United States.

The Caledonia operation expanded in 1979 to include a second plant on the east side of No. 6 highway. Today, it employs approximately two hundred people. The Edinburgh Square Heritage and Cultural Centre at Caledonia's old town hall houses the only museum in North American that claims to tell the story of gypsum. Earl Gillespie, as the Chairman of the Board for the Centre, was instrumental in ensuring that the story of this major company would be available to the public.

There Was Once
a Concert Band

Gone are the days when Caledonia had its own Concert Band. However, there were times when the town just couldn't do without one. Records from as early as 1860 show the existence of a town band. In 1892 it was known as the Fireman's Band and was transported from place to place on the band wagon. During practice the music was supported on high stands equipped with coal-oil lamps. Light for playing at night was provided on the hat of each player or by the light of the moon. A good night's rest often took place in the Band Wagon's straw.

Local boy, Jim Ingles, was a member of that early group. People would speak of hearing his piccola resounding throughout the town as he made his way home to the top of the Catholic Hill from band practise.

Two bandstands were in existence in those days, one at Edinburgh Square and the other in the Gore Park, the name used then for the area where the sixty-seven-year-old Oasis Drive-In stands today, to the south of the bridge.

The town was without a band during the 1930's Depression years until 1947 when the Caledonia Concert Band was organized in January of that year. A modern bandshell went up in 1949 in a picturesque setting along the Grand River.

Adorned in their impressive new uniforms, the musicians marched in parades, with drum majorettes adding flare to the occasion. They put on concerts, competed at the Canadian National Exhibition, played at Garden Parties in Caledonia and throughout the district, entertained at the Caledonia Fair and provided music for dances. Their second place win at the 1955 Canadian National Exhibition, as a result of being tied for first, was considered one of their great accomplishments.

A majority of the musicians had never played an instrument until they joined the band. Professional players, Jim Phillips and Keith Small are still playing the big band music and are often seen playing with the Hamilton Place orchestra.

Found among possessions of Arley Martindale, their business manager, was a list of the top fourteen songs from the 1890's onward. A good part of the Caledonia Concert Band's repertoire was old favourites, including The Sidewalks of New York 1894; The Stars and Stripes Forever 1897; Sweet Adeline 1903; Take Me Out To The Old Ball Game 1908; Ah Sweet Mystery of Life 1910; End of a Perfect Day 1910; When Irish Eyes Are Smiling 1912; St. Louis Blues 1914; Dinah 1925; Ole Man River 1927; Star Dust 1929; Easter Parade 1933; God Bless America 1939; and White Christmas 1942.

The Caledonia Concert Band, led by Eric Small, with two majorettes, Bev Morrison (left) and Helen Mackie, about 1950. The band ceased to exist a decade later.

Letters from World War 1

Clarence and Sydney Hewitt were brothers whose epitaphs denote very different life spans. Clarence Hewitt, a well-known contractor of numerous buildings in Caledonia and area during the early 1900's, lived for almost a century.

One of the buildings, known as the Hewitt Block, was erected in 1927. It stands today just three buildings

Sydney Hewitt.

north of the bridge on the east side of the downtown area. Erected at the same time as the present bridge, it was not the only construction going on in the town at that time. This was an era of revitalization, the economy was booming and Caledonia was once again growing in population.

Clarence Hewitt played a major role in the rejuvenation of Caledonia during the 1920's. Clarence later moved to Burlington and continued to expand his operations. He died in 1987.

His brother, Sydney, however was not so fortunate. His short life spanned only two decades. Tragically, he died in World War 1, at the age of just twenty one while fighting for his country.

The sons of Thomas and Mary Ann (Overend) Hewitt, Clarence and Sydney were born in the late 1800's on a farm in Seneca Township at the Lincoln township boundary line. Records confirm that Sydney left for overseas in March of 1915. His first letter was written on arrival in England, April 19th, 1915 from Ormskirk. A collection of letters was found among Clarence's possessions following his death, by Elsie Felker, a niece of Sydney and Clarence.

Sydney's handwriting was such that his S.S. #9 Seneca schoolteacher would have been proud. His precise and descriptive letters home to Mother tell the story of one World War 1 recruit who went to war full of enthusiasm only to find that it was not a life of glamour and excitement.

Dear Mother:

Well I am in England at last. We got in Liverpool last Saturday at noon, and came to Ormskirk last night. There is only fifteen of the 20th Battalion Transport here.

We left Exhibition grounds two weeks ago last Friday and got in Halifax on the Tuesday with five hundred horses. We had a pretty good trip only it was pretty cold going through Quebec. There being about two feet of snow there yet. We came over here on the Georgia with thirteen hundred and fifty horses, and there was about sixty of us to look after them. We had a fine trip over as far as the weather was concerned, but we got very poor food coming over and we had quite a time looking after the horses. We lost about forty of them on the boat, and we had to throw them overboard and doctor up the sick ones, so we were kept quite busy.

Well I got over without being sea-sick. I felt pretty queer when I was about a day out from Halifax, but did not get sick. About two thirds of the boys were sick for a day, but soon got alright. Well I have to go and answer roll-call now so will finish later.

Well I have got back to writing again. We just had roll-call and are dismissed until two this afternoon. We came over with the biggest cargo that ever crossed the Atlantic. Had 22,000 tons of cargo besides the horses, and fodder for them. We were just eleven days from when we left Halifax until we got in the docks at Liverpool. Liverpool is sure some busy place, with its seven miles of docks. A good part of the supplies that go to France go from there. It is pretty well guarded from air raids. There are machine guns mounted on all the high buildings, and aeroplanes scout over the town on the look-out for raids. After we got in the docks we fed and watered the horses, and then went out and saw the town, we got lost three or four times but we got around all right and found our way back to the boat before midnight.

Yesterday morning there was a fatigue party of soldiers from Seaforth unloaded the horses and put them on the train and sent them out to Lord Derby's estate twelve miles out to a big remount depot. We came out to Ormskirk thirteen miles from Liverpool and three miles from the estate. We are placed in private houses four of us to a house and are just the same as if we were at home. I am at 66 Church Street with three of the boys I chummed (sic) with in Toronto and we are sure in a fine place. We are just like one of the family.

Ormskirk has a population of seven thousand and is just a quiet country town. No-one is in a hurry and they are all friendly. They think quite a lot of the Canadian boys. I have had two or three people ask me for badges, but have got all of them yet. The buildings are a good deal different here than in Canada. They are all made of stone or brick with slate roofs. The streets are made of bricks on cobble stones and are only about half as wide as over there. It certainly is a beautiful place here. The grass is nice and green and some of the flowers are in bloom.

There are no fences, all hedges around the houses and the fields. I don't know if we will have any work to do here or not. We paraded at nine o'clock, and after roll-call were dismissed until two p.m. I think we will stay here until the battalion comes over. I don't know whether they are on there way now or not. We don't know anything that is going on in Canada. There was a bunch of Canadians in this town for three weeks before, and only left on Saturday. I am having some time getting onto the money here. Well, I guess I had better quit or I will have to pay extra postage. The Canadian mail leaves to-morrow so you should get this in ten or twelve days. Write soon.

From
Sydney[29]

The battalion he speaks of was the 114th that left on a Troup Train from Caledonia. The last letter written by Sydney was on Christmas Day, December 25th, 1916.

Dear Mother:

Well mother Xmas day is here once more. It will be a pretty busy day for you, although it is quite enough for me. I am spending the day in a cellar behind the lines, and everything is pretty quiet only a little shelling going on once in a while. The cellar isn't too bad, it is dry and we have beds, if you can call them such, they consist of frames with chicken wire stretched across to lie on. One has to turn over frequently at night to find the soft side of the springs. We have no mattress only a rubber sheet over the wire!

We have just finished our Xmas dinner. We had the quantity if not the quality. It consisted of hash, peas and tomato ketchup, plum pudding and cocoa. The hash was indifferent, the peas were pretty good. The pudding was fair although I failed to find any plums in it, but I got hold of a couple of raisins, so I guess that they ran out of plums and started on the raisins when it was made. I got a fine pudding from Ireland over a week ago, but couldn't carry it around till now so had to eat it. We got a French pie yesterday, and we set it on the stove last night thinking that the rats couldn't get at it there, but we woke up near morning and found it over half gone, so we got up and ate the rest of it, but the rats didn't get much of a feast for it wasn't what it looked to be. The people in this country are not very good cooks.

It is a fine day here, only it is pretty windy, but we don't have any trouble with our hats blowing off for we wear steel helmets all the time,. and they weigh about five pounds so they don't blow around much.

We are in the Reserve now, we don't work in the daytime, but go on working parties every night in the lines, and it sure is some nice job shovelling mud in the dark. I should be used to it by this time, but I can never get to like working at night.

All the fellows that have never been over are all anxious to get over, but when they are over a few weeks, they are all anxious to get back. They think its (sic) fine to be shooting Germans, but unless you make an advance you never see one. I have never fired a shot out of my rifle since last spring. Went through the last trip at the Somme, and never fired a shot. All we do is guards and fatigues. It is fatigue, fatigue all the time shoveling (sic) out trenches and filling sand bags. You just get your line fixed up pretty good and you begin to think you will get a rest, when you are moved to another part, and you have to start all over again.

I am sending you a picture of a bunch of German prisoners taken by this Batt. at the Somme. I didn't get back from England in time to go in the first time, when they captured so many prisoners.

I received C. & C's (Clarence and Cora's) Box a few days ago. The gloves are fine, they are just the kind I wanted. The gloves we get issued with are only cotton ones, and they only last a week or so until they are worn out.

Well mother, I will have to close now. I suppose the big doings will be over and the knot securely tied by now.[30]

> Your loving,
> Sydney[31]

Sidney was killed January 18, 1917. His mother received the following letter written January 28, 1917.

Dear Mrs. Hewitt:
I feel I must write you and express my heartfelt sympathy and condolance in your bereevement. (sic)

I myself feel a keen sense of loss and sorrow, as your son was under my Command on many occasions, and I learnt to value him, not only as an excellant (sic) soldier but also as a solid friend in tight corners.

You will feel comforted to know that he suffered nothing.

Believe me Mrs. Hewitt

> Yours very Sincerly
> J.F. Hannaford, Lieut. Com.

Lieut. Hannaford didn't have the writing nor spelling abilities that Pte. Sydney Hewitt had, but his letter must have been received with sorrow and gracious favour by Sydney's mother who traced every word for safe and precious keeping.

More Stories of Town Life

The Bakery – Caledonia's Oldest Family Business

Albert E. Jones, after receiving his training from the Seldon's Bakery Shop in Caledonia, opened his own store in April 1904. His grandson Hugh along with wife Debbie continue to run the business in the same location and with the same quality standard set by Hugh's grandfather and his father Harold.

Just one year after A.E. Jones acquired the store in August of 1905, a massive explosion of acetylene gas reduced it and the jewellery store next door into a heap of wreckage. It was a Saturday evening and the village's large crowd of Saturday night shoppers hastened toward the terrifying sound of breaking and splintering. The entire front of the large double store had been demolished and fragments of door casings, windows, doors, screens and partitions were strewn across the street. Neighbouring stores were also damaged. The roar of the blast was heard distinctly for miles quite some distance beyond York. Amazingly only twenty-two people were involved in the accident. However, few escaped injury and A.E. Jones had both legs and ankles broken and a heel crushed. He was also severely burned and bruised about the face and hands.

The cause of the explosion was traced to a gas leak that had been noticed for some days, but couldn't be located. At that time, gas was used for the oven in the basement. With the support of businessmen and friends the damage was repaired and business resumed. The first telephone office, before private lines were installed, had been established at the next door jewellery store, but in 1904 following the explosion, was relocated into the bakery. Jones Bakery soon became known as the largest bakery in Haldimand County and the first outside Hamilton to install a bread mixer.

Jones Bakery is the oldest family business still operating in Caledonia. Around the World War II period they operated a fleet of fifteen bread trucks.

With horses and breadwagons and later with a fleet of fifteen bread trucks, Jones Bakery delivered to stores and houses as far away as Hamilton, Brantford, and the rural area surrounding Caledonia through to cottage owners along Lake Erie and Port Dover.

In time Jones Bakery purchased Seldon's Bakery. Now with the total bread business in the area, he employed some twenty-five people. One person was Ed Dietz who continued to deliver bread in town with a horse and bread wagon even after a fleet of trucks were on the road.

The business continued to flourish with A.E.'s son, Harold, joining in 1933. However, in April of 1946, the established family-run operation was sold to Canada Bread Company. The two bakeries were then extended to include larger grocery stock.

A.E. Jones died in 1959. Harold and his wife Jean continued to manage the business

Debbie Jones still uses the original oven.

until 1968 when Harold passed away. By this time their son Hugh had become trained as the baker and maintaining a family tradition, Jean looked after displaying artifacts and pictures of their long established history. She passed away in 1983.

Hugh and his wife, Debbie, went on to create Jones Catering, a very popular wedding, banquet and home party catering service in Caledonia. The family is actively involved also with the Caledonia Fire Department. Hugh has been a long-time member and Debbie is the first woman fire fighter on the staff of the 125-year-old volunteer service organization.

Caledonia's Women's Institute

In May 1906 the Caledonia Senior Women's Institute was formed. After many years of service it disbanded in May of 1943. The branch known as the Caledonia Junior W.I. continued. This Junior group had been organized in February, 1926 following completion of a three month's course in Home Economics. However, in July 1946 the two groups chose to amalgamate under the name of Caledonia Women's Institute.

The Senior W.I. began with a membership of forty-nine and accomplished many improvements for the community. The Women's Institute was instrumental in starting medical inspections in the public schools. A large contribution was made towards the Caledonia Cenotaph in 1922 and they were very active during both World Wars in cooperation with the Red Cross. Among other achievements they had signs erected at each highway entrance in 1930 and in 1939 they procured street signs for the town.

Under their leadership the renovations and redecorating of the Meeting Room at the Town Hall was completed during the 1940's. In more recent years they have contributed to the renovations of the Edinburgh Square and Heritage Centre.

The Tweedsmuir History, begun years ago by the Governor General's wife, Lady Tweedsmuir, as a preservation of local history, is constantly updated by the Caledonia W.I. All original Caledonia Tweedsmuir histories have been placed on microfilm as a permanent record for generations to come.

In the early 1900's, a prominent Caledonia citizen, Joseph Hudspeth, took his pen in hand to write the following poem lampooning the role of husbands whose wives were Institute members. His wife was one of the founding members in Caledonia.

A Husband's View of the Women's Institute

As I sit in the corner and smoke my pipe,
I think the time is almost ripe
For women to wear long pants and a suit
From the wisdom they've gained at the Institute.
The mothers of old spun home-made clothes,
Our sisters mended our broken hose
That our fare was plain I will not dispute,
For we never had heard of an Institute.
Our food was plenty, good, wholesome and clean.
But salads and jellies were never then seen;
Our mothers were housekeepers of some repute
Though nothing was known of an Institute.
But now I am old and unable to roam
I would very much like the comforts of home;
But my wife plays the fiddle and my daughter the Lute
At all the meetings of the Institute.
My shirt is all torn, the buttons are off,
I wash my socks in the old horse trough;
That my wife is busy there is no dispute,
For she is a member of the Institute.
I eat my mush raw and I drink cold tea,
For my wife is busy as she can be
She is writing a paper on canning fruit,
Which she will read at the Institute.
Now I make my own bed and sweep up the floor,
And clean all the rubbish away from the door,
While my wife is at work preparing to shoot
Hot air on the home at the Institute.
When women get votes, as I've no doubt they will,
The first thing they'll do is to pass a new bill
For to make it both lawful and just to shoot,
Or herd all old men in some Institute.
You need not expect me at home for tea,
Was the parting salute my wife gave me
We are having a lady of some repute
To lecture today at the Institute.
There are cold potatoes on the pantry shelf
If you find anything else just help yourself.
The lady comes prepared to refute
All charges made against the Institute.

Dentistry of Another Era

An off-told story from the 1880's explains how Sandy Lawson, a local tailor, practised dentistry. One summer afternoon Sandy strolled down Caithness Street with the idea of enjoying a chat with his old friend, Dr. Burns, a general medical practitioner. The door was open, but the doctor was out on a case. Sandy settled down in a comfortable chair and picked up a magazine, making himself at home. Hearing footsteps, he naturally thought it was the doctor returning, but suddenly realized it was a farmer who had recently moved into the district.

"I'm sair wi' an awful toothache. Is the doctor in?" gasped the farmer.
"Certainly," said Sandy. "What can I do for you."
"Ye can pul this d.......d tooth, is what ye can do."
Frequent visits to the doctor's office had given Sandy the location of the instruments the doctor used and Sandy appeared from the back room with the forceps. In a professional manner, he held back the forehead of the farmer, adjusted the forceps on the troublesome tooth, and with a powerful pull, the molar was held in the face of the farmer.
"That's fine," he said, "hoo much do I owe ye?"
"Oh," said Sandy, "Fifty cents, will be all right."
Sandy quickly put the money in his pocket and henceforth, proud as a peacock, told how he once practised dentistry.

Thousands Are Called Home in 1927

The Dominion Day holiday in 1927 called thousands home to Caledonia for the Old Boys and Girls Reunion, designed to mark the 60th Anniversary of Confederation. They came from all over Canada, the United States and England to take part in a well-planned five day celebration. Enticed by reduced train fares, sports events, dancing, a garden party, Church services, tours, Indian Dances and a Callithumpian parade, it was an advertised occasion not to be missed. A candidate for the Miss Canada contest was also to be selected as part of the festivities.

Bruce French, the local historian, wrote a detailed history; Ob Scott, the millowner, wrote poetry and Mrs. Sawle, publisher of *The Sachem*, put out a five-thousand plus run of a Souvenir edition for regular subscribers, non subscribers and the returning "old boys and girls." That June 1, 1927 edition has been used extensively for historic research ever since. Scott's ten verse poem entitled "The Call" headed the front page. It began with:

> The old Town's call is sounding
> To sons and daughters dear -
> You, who have left the Village,
> And scattered, far and near -
> Come Home – we want to see you,
> Come Home – there's room – no fear,
> Come, celebrate this year.

At 4 a.m. on Friday, July 1, 1927, the blowing of whistles and the noise of guns gave the signal to commence. The downtown business area, the Town Hall and private homes had all been decorated with flags and bunting. The setting was described as "an atmosphere of happiness everywhere"[32]

The Callithumpian Parade, followed by crowds in cars and on foot, met the Toronto contingent at the train station. Toronto's own organization, "The Caledonia Old Boys and Girls Association of Toronto" headed by Walter Seldon, disembarked the train to the strains of "Home Sweet Home". They proceeded down the street with their badges and gaily coloured swagger sticks to Edinburgh Square for the awarding of prizes.

That was the beginning of the five-day affair. Friday was billed as Dominion Day; Saturday, Haldimand County Day; Sunday, Devotional Day; Monday, American Day and Tuesday, Fireman's Day. For each day an agenda of events was prominently displayed.

For weeks following the newspaper listed registered homecomers and "I Remember" columns continued to be published. Ob Scott's "The Answer" began this way:

> The Home Town's call has sounded-
> 'Tis answered loud and clear
> O how its offspring gathered,
> Coming from far and near.

> Wide were the doors thrown open,
> Oh how they hastened here
> These boys and girls, these pals and chums,
> The "KIDS" of yesteryear.

Although the Federal Government had proclaimed three days of legal holiday to celebrate the Diamond Anniversary, there seemed to have been some confusion as to what was expected of the local merchants. Two holidays were to precede the Sunday. However, it was not possible at that time of year to buy sufficient supplies to last over the three days,

Edinburgh Square at the time of the 1927 Diamond Jubilee celebrations.

not to mention meeting the needs of the added company settled in each household for the celebration. Most towns adopted the rule that merchants would be open Saturday, so Caledonia followed.

The Jubilee extravaganza went far beyond expectation. Although this was the beginning of many annual celebrations on Dominion Day, festivities were not repeated again on such a large scale until 1950 when Haldimand County's Centennial celebrations took place. Since 1992 when Canada celebrated its 125 anniversary, Canada Day events in Caledonia continue to attract enthusiastic crowds.

An Anniversary Broadcast

In recognition of the 100th Anniversary of the town's only newspaper, *The Grand River Sachem*, CBC's popular Sunday morning radio program "Neighbourly News" saluted Caledonia and Haldimand County on February 6, 1956. By 9:45 a.m. a large crowd had gathered in the Town Hall's upper floor to participate in the special Centennial broadcast hosted by CBC radio personalities Don Fairbairn and Bill Bessey. Among the noted special guests were: Haldimand County Judge, Helen Kinnear; Crown Attorney, Harrison Arrell; Ontario Minister of Highways, Hon. James Allan; Warden. Lloyd Baker; Reeve, William Winegard; High School Principal, T.J. Hicks; and Rural Postman, Arthur Bain.

Helen Kinnear, the first woman KC in Canada and the only female Judge in the British Commonwealth, stated that she felt women should serve on juries. "In fact I think women should play a much more active role in public life than they do," she said. "There are many fields in both municipal and national areas where a woman's knowledge and advice could be extremely valuable."[33]

Crown Attorney Harrison Arrell, then eighty-two years of age, had practised law in Caledonia since before the turn of century and was still the County Clerk and County Solicitor. In recalling his coming to Caledonia in 1885, he noted changes that had occurred since then. "The population was 800 people and a large number of cows and horses, all roamed the streets

Judge Helen Kinnear, born in Cayuga, was appointed to the Bench in 1943.

at will and with board sidewalks this caused a great deal of confusion."[34] He went on to tell of a proposed by-law to prohibit cattle running at large being a lively issue at election time. It split the town into two camps, but supporters of the new by-law won and since then cattle have been fenced in.

Reeve Winegard spoke of the main street being resurfaced the year before in 1955 and the findings when it was torn up. "The old Plank Road from Hamilton to Port Dover went down our main street and when we tore it up last fall we found many of the original planks, most in good condition. They were two or three inches thick, eighteen inches wide and up to 16 feet long."[35]

Harrison Arrell, Q.C., born near Onondaga, played a major role in the life of Caledonia and Haldimand County for over sixty years.

The radio program was a momentous occasion for the community and for the *Grand River Sachem*. Local history of their small Ontario town, similar to the towns known by many who were regular listeners of "Neighbourly News", was being recorded for all to hear.

Hockey Popularity

In 1962 the Caledonia Corvair Hockey Club came into being as an indirect out-growth of Church League hockey. Today the club is as well-known in Ontario Hockey Association circles as it is at home. The name has something to do with it. Unlike Terriers, Blazers or Rangers, the name choice for Caledonia's new hockey club in 1961 was to be Corvairs.

The club founders, Bud Miller, Ches Martindale and Dave Peirson, counted on needed funding from the local Wills Chev/Olds dealership. Corvair, the new Chevy compact featured at the time, seemed to be an appropriate name to coerce the dealership into parting with dollars. As it turned out, a $300 cheque was the only sponsorship required. The name no longer is thought of as a car to Caledonians, but as a hockey team.

1968-69 Corvair Champions. Back row, left to right – Terry McLean, Bob Martin, Ches Martindale, Dave Peirson, Bruce Hudspeth, Bob McMaster, Bud Miller, Reg Peirson, Dr. Wally Landers. Centre row – Brent Shipway, Danny Richards, Brone Serblan, Stan Wolkowski, John Winegard, Tom Misener, Tom Young, Brian Etherington, Al Lickers, Bob Moerschfelder, Cliff Lickers. Front row – Gary Blackwell, Dennis Davey, Bob Archer, Ken Murray, Paul Denaegal, Bob Gilman, Peter Parker, Jim Parker.

A pre-Corvairs hockey team. Handwritten caption on the back of the photo lists members as follows: Harvey Longboat, Tom Davey, Bob Guyatt, "Whitey" Lawrence Whitelaw, Jim Harris, George Draper, Fred Helka, Ron Smith, Bill Brown, Roy Edwards, Don Edwards, Roland Jenkins, Don Emerson and Victor Porter.

The popularity of the Corvairs grew as the result of a marketing technique targeting new and different ideas for the 1960's. A certain dedication evolved from a hardworking and faithful executive body and from the fans who took pride in the Corvairs success. The management treated their players with respect and expected the same in return. As a result, discipline was not difficult. A ruling that players had to wear a shirt and tie to all games indicated, in days of the more relaxed dress code, that management meant business. This new approach to Junior small town hockey was incorporated from a Lambeth team they had played in a championship series.

Raising funds to carry them through a season was always a serious priority that took time and effort. Game receipts could be counted on to break even more often than showing a profit when referees, ice rental, pucks and other necessities were added to the cost of running a team. Sweaters, socks, pads, pants and hockey sticks were additional major expenses. When other clubs were expecting their players to have their own equipment, the Corvairs Hockey Club provided for their players.

Creation of a positive successful profile in hockey led to their bringing a team to town from across the American border. This experience was both an education for each player and a crowd pleaser. Fort Wayne, Indiana was welcomed with open arms and noticeable preparation by all. Before long before the invitation was returned and the Caledonia team was truly recognized.

Caledonians of the 1960's and early 70's considered the Corvair Dances in the arena to be the one annual event not to miss on the Saturday night after Labour Day. Big band music was the key to a good time where crowds of 1,000 people rocked inside the old arena walls. Those dances were even more popular during the days when a Miss Corvair was crowned. With the title each year, the honour included automatic entry in the Miss Tiger Cat competition.

An Ontario Junior D Championship in 1969 and an Ontario Junior C Championship in 1972 have never been equalled. The old arena in 1969 drew overwhelming crowds for the final games and fans literally hung from the rafters to cheer their team on to victory. The 1972 championship games in the new arena provided more comfortable surroundings and an even larger seating capacity for the enthusiastic followers.

A group of cheerleaders found their spot behind the bench during the early 1970's and were a colourful addition to a game that didn't ordinarily lend itself to cheerleaders.

Along with the happy times and the fun of team involvement were sad times too. Team members, John Haller, Alvin Locker and Tommy Spratt, were unfortunately killed in accidents on separate occasions. Their sweater numbers were put to rest with each of them. Co-founder and coach, Chester Martindale, in February 1980 also met his untimely death as the result of a car accident following that hockey season's end.

While management and players have changed over the years, the Corvair Hockey Club retains its stature in Junior hockey circles and among Caledonia fans. Co-founder Bud Miller was Manager for twenty-six years and was a member on the Ontario Hockey Association Executive for ten years.

Hundreds of Caledonia and area boys have graduated from the Minor Hockey system to play for the Corvairs. Many have gone on to play university hockey and some to other hockey endeavours. One in particular, Don Edwards, the Caledonia goalie for the 1972 Championship team, achieved the goal of many young Ontario boys by making it to the National Hockey League. A distinction also shared by his uncle, Roy.

Baseball

Baseball as an organized sport began in Caledonia in 1918. On a snow-covered field in Peterborough in 1921, the intermediate team was defeated for the provincial crown by Picton. From then on Caledonia had either an intermediate or a junior team that remained at the top.

When the war broke out, baseball came to a halt, but the old spirit was revived when the boys returned from battle and by 1948 they were champions. They took the Ontario crown in an exciting final game against

Caledonia Baseball Club, 1948 Ontario Intermediate "C" Champions. Standing, left to right – W. Moyer, coach; A.E. Jones, hon. pres.; W. Clark; W. Gordon; W. Morrison; N. Pottruff; G. Fedoroko; R. Harrison; S. Thompson; F. Gyokery; A. Gibb; R. Gordon, manager. Front row – R. Smith; K. Neilson, Captain; E. Sabo; R. Moffat; F. Sabo; H. Shea; D. Morrison; E. Ahonpa.

Clinton and returned home to a gathering of the whole town at the main corner, where a bonfire was the focal point of the hoopla.

Minor baseball was not organized until the spring of 1947, when Roy Spratt, Ed Dietz, Earl Winger, Eino Mackie and Tom Morrison formed the first executive. Three teams were formed in the town league and after a successful season picked a team from the three with great promise to represent Haldimand in the OBA playoffs. They were eliminated by Tillsonburg.

A bantam team was organized and added in 1949 and by 1950 there was also a midget team.

Today baseball is growing in popularity in Caledonia, from T-ballers to intermediates. There is also a softball league. The only ball diamond for many years was at Edinburgh Square, and it is still in regular use. The Ed Dietz diamond at Lions Park has two ball fields along with a soccer field, and there is a diamond at Kinsmen Park too. The new Henning Park, north of Caledonia on Green's Road, has two diamonds now, with a third almost ready and plans for a fourth.

The Day the Ice Goes Out

The breaking up of the ice in the Grand River was always looked forward to with anticipation, and more often than not, some concern for potential extensive damage. Now that the Grand River Conservation Authority has control over the waters, the thrill and the threat fortunately are gone.

In 1861 the ice caused severe damage when the spring freshet, as they referred to it, moved the McKinnon sawmill five feet away from its original location. A jam of ice and timber, together with a scow piled as high as the roof of the sawmill, rushed over the dam. It wiped out the Caledonia bridge and rushed further down to destroy the Seneca Bridge that crossed the Grand River. That bridge was never replaced. The flooding of the old village of Seneca sent people to the second stories of their homes.

It happened again in 1874 and in numerous years intermittently thereafter, until 1976 when the worst flood of more recent years completely put the fairgrounds and many store basements under water. A new dam at Caledonia in 1980, a modern water control structure, along with stepped-up control of the entire Grand River system by the Grand River Conservation Authority has virtually eliminated flooding today.

Service Clubs used the excitement of the ice going out as an occasion to raise money by putting a date and time to the breaking up of ice flowing over the dam. Tickets were sold on a 45 gallon drum placed on a raft in the Grand River just below the bypass bridge west of the dam. The trick was to name the correct month, day, hour and minute the ice would break up enough to carry the raft over the dam and under the bridge. Today, the ice goes out unnoticed except by those who remember the days of old and who still gather along the banks to watch.

The old original Caledonia Dam in disrepair (right). The new Caledonia Dam (below) replaced it in 1980.

Big Creek Boat Farm

John and Luella Albin thought the Grand River Navigation era was one that could be repeated in some way. They believed they could see the potential held by the sleeping Grand.

On June 21, 1978, with the smash of a bottle of champagne, they launched the *Grand River Belle*. It took the help of about a dozen men and a crowd of friends and neighbours to get their replica of the navigation days vessel into the quiet waters. This launch was the beginning of more to come. To this day Caledonians look to the Albin's venture as one of the area's most successful entrepreneurial businesses.

The *Grand River Belle* doesn't travel much faster than those river boats

Big Creek Boat Farm's *Grand River Belle*, the first riverboat to ply the Grand River since the demise of the Grand River Navigation Company..

of the century before. The best of them were reputed to take an hour to travel ten miles, sometimes more if they were going against the current. The *Grand River Belle* leisurely sets the same speed while the captain informally relays interesting history to passengers who are dining while they cruise. The year 1983 saw more than 100,000 people cruising the Grand and interest continues to grow. The Albin's dream has come a long way since the first launch in 1978.

By 1984 the *Grand River Belle* had acquired "offspring" when the *Grand River Queen* and *Grand River Princess* began cruising the waters of the Grand. Visitors by the busloads were arriving from across the United States as well as from Southern Ontario. The Big Creek Boat Farm was re-establishing navigation along the Grand.

This success led to creating "The Loft" in a converted century old barn standing on their property. With dinner theatre in a rustic atmosphere, gift shops on one side and a bakery on the other, new life was appearing as fun for the visitors and employment opportunities for local people. Young people aspiring to theatre careers staged the productions and waited on the tables. Until 1986, a special Christmas show attracted thousands over its three week production.

Today Big Creek Boat Farm with a staff of thirty people is a major attraction at Caledonia. The Six Nations Reserve plays a major role in its appeal as well. A bus tour of the Six Nations Reserve can be taken from Big Creek Boat Farm and the *Lady Onondaga* is an added feature to the cruise line. A craft shop on the Six Nations Reserve, across the Grand River from Chiefswood Park, is a stop-over for passengers wanting to pick up souvenirs from the area. The Grand River still attracts attention and contributes to the livelihood of its towns and villages.

Big Creek Boat Farm entertainers, captains, and owners John and Luella Albin (centre front).

Caledonia Scenes...

Above: Caledonia's nine-span bridge.

Left: The Haldimand Choralairs, founded by the late George Shippey in 1967, shown entertaining at Cayuga Seconday School in 1984.

Below: Generations of Caledonians have enjoyed the annual Santa Claus parade, held in late November.

The Canada Day Parade in 1994. Shown in the carriage are Slim Norseworthy and Mayor Marie Trainer.

Below: Generations of Caledonians have served their country over the years.

Above: Soccer has been gaining in popularity among young people over the past few years.

Right: A close-up of the fish ladder that allows spawning fish to go around the dam.

Memories

by O.T. Scott, 1956

I can't go back one hundred years
And from my memory bring
Fond pictures of our Village then,
I cannot tell a thing.
My earliest recollections start
In eighteen eighty-five,
I lived up on the Catholic Hill
A little boy of five.
The hill is not as steep to-day,
In winter time my sleigh
Would scoot across the sidewalk
And on the Square away.
The Priest, he had an Orchard,
The picket fence a hole,
Sometimes we asked, sometimes we failed,
He was a kindly soul.
We all kept cows, they roamed the streets,
From School we had to roam
The Village o'er before we found
And brought those bovine home.
The streets were mud, the Plank Road gone,
But in the springtime rain
Those planks got resurrection hopes
And up they came again.
The sidewalks all were made of Plank,
The ladies' skirts were long,
The nails worked up and tore those skirts,
The Council got in wrong.

We had a dandy swimmin' hole,
Straight down from the Town Hall,
The kid that swam out to THE ROCK
Was champion of all.
The fishing at the Dam was great,
The Slab Piles lined the shore,
We bobbed for Bass and trolled for Pike,
Then waded out for more.
In winter time the River froze
Quite thick from shore to shore,
The Farmers used it as a Road
For several months and more,
They cut their Ice above the Dam
To last the summer through,
While we boys played our Shinny Game
And watched the process through,
To "Hang on Bobs" was one great sport
We practised far and wide,
We'd ride the Farmers' sleighs for miles
Then catch a homeward ride.
At Trotter's we got Licorice Root,
And Roper's sold us Pills,
While Doctor Forbes and Doctor Burns
Cured all our childhood ills.
I well recall our first Gas Well,
Behind Fred Avery's shop,
And what it did to our Cook Stove
In twisting up its top.
They charged a Dollar every month
For each Stove we did burn,
Boy – when I get my Gas Bills now
For those good days I yearn.
I went each day to Seldon's Store
To get our daily bread,
It smelled so good I nibbled some,
You guess what Mother said.
I can't forget that Blacksmith Shop
Where Billy S held sway,

He fixed my broken toys and tools,
And always yelled "Good Day"
The Village Square was much the same,
The Cows mowed long grass short,
We had our Baseball, Cricket too,
Our days were filled with sport.
These golden days have passed away,
Old friends are leaving me,
And yet I do not wish them back,
The best is yet to be.
Life's day brought joys and sorrow,
My maker planned it so;
But early morning's beauties
Can't match the Sunset's glow.

Notes and Picture Credits

1. The prefix "Teh" seen all the way through, in Indian history, means, Two, Dual Nature - Lord and War Lord. Teyoninhokarawen signifies "open door", importing, frankness and an open heart. His native name was given to him when he was appointed chief and would signifiy him as both a Civil and War chief.*The Journal of Major John Norton, 1816.* The Champlain Society of Canada, 1970.
2. The Champlain Society of Canada was founded in 1905. Sir Byron Edmund Walker, also profiled in this book, was its first president. It was established to publish journals of history scholars.
3. *The Journal of Major John Norton 1816.* The Champlain Society of Canada, 1970.
4. It is interesting to note that Perth, Ontario claims the last fatal duel in 1833.
5. *The Journal of Major John Norton 1816.* The Champlain Society of Canada, 1970.
6. Ibid
7. Ibid
8. *A Guide to the Grand River Canal,* St. Catharines Historical Museum, 1981.
9. Colin K. DuQuemin, *A Guide to the Grand River Canal.* St. Catherines Historical Museum. 1981
10. Alex Arrell, *A History of Caledonia,* The Grand River Sachem. 1950
11. Anne Corlis, *Caledonia and District, A History,* Caledonia Women's Institute. 1959
12. *The Grand River Sachem,* December 2, 1858.
13. Jessie MacGregor brochure; Edinburgh Square Heritage & Cultural Centre
14. Ibid
15. Ibid
16. Ibid
17. *People of the community, Our Town Hall,* Town of Haldimand Museum Board, 1982
18. Taped conversation between Rev. McMillan and Warren Clark, Edinburgh Square Heritage and Cultural Centre Collections of oral history, 1987.
19. Ibid
20. *The Grand River Sachem,* 100th Anniversary Souvenir Edition, February, 1956

21. Mohawk translation, "Greetings and how are you/are you well?" Translation courtesy of Ontario Federation of Indian Friendship Centres.

22. Joseph Schull, *Ontario Since 1867*, McLelland and Stewart, 1978, page 121

23. Joseph Schull, *Ontario Since 1867*, McLelland and Stewart, 1978, page 201.

24. Harrison Martindale, *The Grand River Sachem*; November 28, 1979.

25. The John Gilpin ride reference is from a humorous ballad by William Cowper, written in 1782 about John Gilpin's ride on horseback. Being a bad rider, Gilpin grasps the mane with both hands. On goes the horse and off flies John Gilpin's cloak, together with his hat and wig.

26. *Caledonia Advertiser*, March 12, 1856.

27. J. George Johnston, *The Weeklies*, The Bolton Enterprise, 1972, page 92.

28. Taped conversation between Earl Gillespie and Barbara Martindale, Edinburgh Square Heritage and Cultural Centre, 1989.

29. Sydney Hewitt letters compiled by Elsie Felker; Edinburgh Square Heritage and Cultural Centre, 1991.

30. This is in reference to his sister Josie who had just married.

31. Sydney Hewitt letters.

32. *The Grand River Sachem*, July 13, 1927.

33. CBC Neighbourly News, February 6, 1956 written transcript, Edinburgh Square Heritage and Cultural Centre

34. Ibid

35. Ibid

Picture Credits

The picture of the old Town Hall above the chapter titles is used courtesy of Edinburgh Square Heritage and Cultural Centre.

2   *Grand River Sachem*.

6   *Grand River Sachem*.

12   Edinburgh Square Heritage and Cultural Centre.

14   *Grand River Sachem*.

15   National Gallery of Canada painting.

16   Haldimand County Museum, Cayuga.

17   Portrait by Thomas Phillips, R.D. *The Journal of Major John Horton 1814*, Toronto, The Champlain Society, 1970.

19   Jean McClung.

25   Robin McKee.

26   Bill Balsdon Collection.

27   Edinburgh Square Heritage and Cultural Centre.

29   Private postcard, Gorman & Co., Caledonia, Edinburgh Square Heritage and Cultural Centre.

30   Author's private collection.

31   Upper photo: *Grand River Sachem*.

31 Lower photo: Pen and ink reproduction by George Rickard Studio, London, Ont.
32 *Grand River Sachem*.
33 Edinburgh Square Heritage and Cultural Centre.
34 *Grand River Sachem*.
35 Haldimand County Museum, Cayuga.
37 Haldimand County Museum, Cayuga.
40 Les Richardson collection.
41 Les Richardson collection.
43 Edinburgh Square Heritage and Cultural Centre.
44 Edinburgh Square Heritage and Cultural Centre.
45 Edinburgh Square Heritage and Cultural Centre.
47 Edinburgh Square Heritage and Cultural Centre.
50 Upper photo: Hubert Beckett, Hamilton, Ont., courtesy of Doug Scott.
50 Lower photo: Edinburgh Square Heritage and Cultural Centre.
51 Jean McClung.
53 Mrs. Patrick Sullivan (Marlene Heddle).
54 Reproduced from 1955 Six Nations Pageant booklet.
55 Author's private collection.
56 Author's private collection.
60 Author's private collection.
61 Upper photo: Author's private collection.
61 Lower photo: Courtesy Pearl Ilett.
62 Frank Szabo.
63 Bill Balsdon collection.
65 Upper photo: Woodland Cultural Education Centre.
65 Lower photo: Edinburgh Square Heritage and Cultural Centre.
66 Upper photo: Woodland Cultural Education Centre.
66 Lower photo: Woodland Cultural Education Centre.
68 Betsy Smith (Small),Cayuga.
69 Private postcard, McGregor & Co., Caledonia (Made in Germany), Author's private collection.
70 Jean McClung.
71 Edinburgh Square Heritage and Cultural Centre.
72 *Grand River Sachem*.
73 Jean McClung.
75 Haldimand County Museum, Cayuga.
76 Edinburgh Square Heritage and Cultural Centre.
77 Edinburgh Square Heritage and Cultural Centre.
78 Edinburgh Square Heritage and Cultural Centre.
79 Jean McClung.
81 Author's private collection.
·82 Upper photo: Author's private collection.

82 Lower engraving: Edinburgh Square Heritage and Cultural Centre.

83 *Grand River Sachem.*

85 Edinburgh Square Heritage and Cultural Centre.

86 Author's private collection.

87 Edinburgh Square Heritage and Cultural Centre.

91 Elsie Felker (Binbrook).

96 Upper photo: Jones Bakery.

96 Lower photo: *Grand River Sachem..*

101 Private postcard, McGregor & Co., Caledonia, Edinburgh Square Heritage and Cultural Centre.

102 Upper photo: Haldimand Press, Hagersville.

102 Lower photo: *Grand River Sachem..*

103 Photo by Herb Smith, Simcoe, Author's private collection.

104 *Grand River Sachem.*

106 *Grand River Sachem.*

107 Jean McClung.

107 Inset photo: Stephen Halfpenny.

108 *Grand River Sachem.*

109 Jean McClung.

110 All: *Grand River Sachem.*

111 All: *Grand River Sachem*

Acknowledgments & Information

Museums

Edinburgh Square Heritage and Cultural Centre, Caledonia
Haldimand County Museum, Cayuga
Ontario Agricultural Museum, Milton

Individuals

Mary Nelles
Earl Gillespie
Harrison Martindale
Barbra Lang Walker
Jean McClung (photographs)
Robin McKee (photographs)
Volunteers of Edinburgh Square Heritage and Cultural Centre, and many, many others who on behalf of their families contributed information.

For More Information

Edinburgh Square Heritage and Cultural Centre
74 Edinburgh Square, P.O. Box 2056
Caledonia, Ontario N3W 2G6

The Town of Haldimand
P.O. Box 400
Cayuga, Ontario N0A 1E0

The Haldimand County Museum
Munsee Street
Cayuga, Ontario N0A 1E0

The Caledonia Public Library
35 Caithness Street West
Caledonia, Ontario N3W 1B7

Sources

Arrell, Alex H., editor; *A Short History of Caledonia*; The Grand River Sachem Printing, 1950.

Caledonia Advertiser; Feb.-Nov. 1856.

Caledonia, *The Grand River Sachem*; since November 19, 1856.

Choquet, Robert; *Ontario, An Informal History of the Land and Its People*; Ontario Ministry of Education, Ontario Ministry of Colleges and Universities; 1984.

Corlis, Anne; *Caledonia and District, a History 1959, Tweedsmuir History*, Caledonia Women's Institute; self-published; 1959.

DuQuemin, Colin K; *A Guide to the Grand River Canal*; St. Catharines Historical Museum; 1981.

Harper, Russell; *The Early History of Haldimand County*; The Grand River Sachem Printing, 1950.

Gillespie, Evelyn and Anne Corlis and Isobel Smith; *Caledonia's Century Homes*; self-published, 1967.

Harper, Russell; *The Early History of Haldimand County*; The Grand River Sachem Printing, 1950.

Harris, R. Cole and John Warkentin; *Ontario Before Confederation*; Oxford University Press, 1974.

Johnston, J. George; *The Weeklies*; The Bolton Enterprise printing; 1972.

Klinck, Carl F. and James J. Talman; *The Journal of Major John Norton 1816*; The Champlain Society, 1970.

Neighbourly News; CBC Radio written transcript; February 6, 1956.

Our Town Hall; Town of Haldimand Museum Board; self-published; 1982.

Quinsey, William John; *York, Grand River, Its Early History and Directory 1834-1860*; The York Grand River Historical Society, 1991.

Seneca Centennial Historical Committee; *The Township of Seneca History 1867-1967*; The Grand River Sachem printing; 1967.

Schull, Joseph; *Ontario Since 1867*; McClelland and Stewart; 1978.

The Grand Strategy for Managing the Grand River as a Canadian Heritage River; Coordinated by The Grand River Conservation Authority on behalf of the Province of Ontario; 1994.

Index

Addison, Robert (Reverend), 18, 19
Alatint, 87
Albin, Luella, 108, 109
Albin, John, 108, 109
Ahonpa, E., 106
Alexander, Alexander, 59
Alexander, Mary (Lady Walker), 59
Allen, James (Hon.), 101
Almonte Fall Fair, 48
Ames, Mrs. Emily (Sawle), 65
American Revolution, 15
Apps Mill (Paris), 79
Argyle Street, 17, 30, 38, 41, 43, 46, 50, 53, 60, 67
Archer, Bob, 103
Argyle Heights Apartments, 53
Arrell, Harrison (Barrister), 44, 101, 102
Arrell, Mrs. Harrison (Eva Sawle), 65
Avery, S., 68
Ayr, 50

Bain, Arthur, 101
Bain, Charles, 21
Baker, Lloyd, 101
Balmoral Mill, 41, 42
Bank of Hamilton, 44
Bay, Lydia (Mrs. J. Beaver), 65
Bearfoot Village, 20
Beaver, Jim (Chief), 64, 65, 66
Beaver's Corners, 64, 65
Bell, Alexander Graham, 54, 55
Bennett, Richard D. (Prime Minister), 53
Bessey, Bill, 101
Big Arrow, Joseph, 20, 21
Big Creek Boat Farm, 108, 109
Black Creek, 78

Black Creek Bridge, 77
Blackwell, Gary, 103
Boose's Drug Store, 62
Borden, Robert Laird (Prime Minister), 52, 59
Brant, Joseph (Chief), 15, 18
Brantford, 16, 17, 22, 23, 24, 31, 53, 54, 55, 64, 69, 96
Brantford (tugboat), 23
Britton, Bridget, 40
Brown, Bill, 104
Brown, George, 36
Bryant, Mr., 17, 35, 43
Bryant's Corners, 17
Bryant's Tavern, 17, 43
Buffalo (New York), 26, 82
Buffalo, Brantford & Goderich Railroad, 26
Builder, John, 84
Burlington, 91
Burns, Dr., 99

CBC, 101
Caithness Street, 17, 38, 39, 43, 46, 50, 60, 62, 82, 83, 99
Caledonia (freight boat), 24
Caledonia Advisor, 81
Caledonia Agriculture and Art Society, 32, 33, 34, 67
Caledonia Band Shell, 68, 89
Caledonia Baseball Club, 106
Caledonia Bridge, 13, 73, 79, 80
Caledonia Chapter 236, 44
Caledonia Citizen Band, 74
Caledonia Concert Band, 89, 90
Caledonia Corvair Hockey Club, 103,

104, 105
Caledonia Dam, 106, 107
Caledonia Fair, 30, 32, 33, 67, 68, 69, 89
Caledonia Fire Brigade, 74, 98
Caledonia Foundry and Iron Works
  (Scott Foundry), 84, 85
Caledonia High School, 52
Caledonia Horticultural Society, 67
Caledonia Junior Women's Institute, 97
Caledonia Mill (Old Mill), 41, 78, 79
Caledonia Milling Company, 41, 50, 51,
  77, 79
Caledonia Presbyterian Church, 38, 42, 52
Caledonia Railway Station, 28, 30, 31,
  34, 37, 48
Caledonia Rifles, 67
Caledonia Senior Women's Institute, 97
Caledonia Women's Institute, 97, 98
Campbell House Hotel, 28
Canada Bread Company, 96
Canadian Bank of Commerce, 58, 59
Canadian Forestry Association, 42
Canadian Gypsum Company, 85
Canadian Heritage River, 14, 26
Canadian Illustrated News, 85
Canadian National Exhibition, 89
Canadian Magazine, 56
Carpenter, Walter, 39
Caroline Messmore (tugboat), 23
Cayuga, 13, 16, 22, 24, 25, 30, 41, 45, 71,
  81
Cayuga Sachem, 81
Cenotaph, 67, 69, 97
Champlain Society of Canada, 17, 18, 20,
  58
Chautauqua, 44, 49, 71
Cherokee, 17, 18, 21
Chiefswood, 54, 55
Chiefswood Museum, 57
Chiefswood Park, 109
Church of England, 19
Christ Church, 65
Clark, W., 106
Conestoga River, 26
Crawford, Joe (Joseph Big Arrow), 21
Crealock, A.B., 74
Creighton, J.H., 77
Culp, Bill, 63
Culp, Lizzie, 63

Culp, Lloyd A. (Tuffy), 63, 64

Davey, Dennis, 103
Davey, Tom, 104
Denaegal, Paul, 103
Diamond Anniversary (Jubilee), 53, 60,
  61, 100, 101
Delhi, 83
Dietz, Ed, 96, 106
Domtar, 86, 88
Donaghy, C., 68
Doughty, Alma (Mrs. O.T. Scott), 50, 51
Doyle, William (Bill, Billy), 60
Doyle, William (Constable), 60
Doxtador, Alta, 65
Draper, George, 104
Drill Hall (Glasgow Hall), 67, 68
Dufferin County, 15, 26
Duke of Northumberland (2nd), 18
Duke of Northumberland (3rd), 20
Duke of Northumberland (10th), 18
Dunnville, 16
Dunnville Dam, 16

Eadie, Effie, 39
Eadie, Flora (McKinnon), 39
Edinburgh Square, 13, 32, 49, 61, 67, 68,
  69, 84, 89, 100
Edinburgh Square Heritage and Cultural
  Centre, 65, 66, 70, 71, 72, 73, 84, 88, 97
Edwards, Don, 104, 105
Edwards, Roy, 104, 105
Elgar Ladies, 47
Elliott, W.E., 46
Emerson, Don, 104
Emerson, T., 68
England, 17, 58, 87, 88, 99
Eramosa River, 26
Etherington, Brian, 103
Esquising, 36

Fairbairn, Doug, 101
Farnsworth, S.H., 23
Fedoroko, G., 106
Fedro, James, 82
Felker, Elsie, 91
Five Nations, 18
Fleet Aircraft, 88
Fleming, Etta, 61, 62

Fleming, Wesley, 61, 62
Forster, M.E. (Variety Store), 44
French, Bruce E., 60, 61, 74, 99
French, Flo (Florence Lawson), 61
French, Helen, 61

Gibb, A., 106
Gillespie Clark Library Resource Centre, 72
Gillespie, Earl, 63, 85, 86, 87, 88
Gilman, Bob, 103
Glasgow Square, 67
Goderich, 26, 46
Golden Horsehow Antique Society, 78
Gore Park, 89
Gordon, R., 106
Gordon, W., 106
Gorman & Co., 30
Grand River, 13, 14, 15, 16, 17, 19, 20, 26, 27, 28, 34, 54, 55, 64, 71, 75, 78, 80, 82, 85, 86, 89, 106, 107, 108, 109
Grand River Belle (river boat), 108, 109
Grand River Canal, 23
Grand River Conservation Authority, 79, 106, 107
Grand River Mills, 41
Grand River Navigation Company, 16, 22, 24, 25, 28, 29, 36, 40, 108
Grand River Princess (river boat), 109
Grand River Queen (river boat), 109
Grand River Sachem, 34, 38, 53, 60, 61, 63, 65, 73, 74, 81, 82, 83, 99, 101, 103
Great Western Railway, 26
Greenock Square, 67
Guyatt, Bob, 104
Gyokery, F., 106

Hagersville, 13, 36, 63, 85
Haldimand Agricultural Society, 32
Haldimand Choralairs, 110
Haldimand County, 13, 24, 32, 40, 43, 44, 53, 80, 86, 95, 100, 101, 102, 106
Haldimand, Grant, 14, 15, 16, 24
Haldimand House, 40, 41, 63
Haldimand Navigation Company, 24, 75
Haldimand, Sir Frederick, 15, 16
Haller, John, 105
Hambourg, Mark, 46
Hamilton, 14, 28, 30, 34, 35, 42, 57, 59, 85, 88, 95, 96, 102
Hamilton and Port Dover Line, 27, 28, 41
Hamilton Bridge Works, 77
Hamilton Central Fairgrounds, 32
Hamilton Mountain, 36, 41
Hamilton Spectator (The), 34
Hamilton Place, 90
Hambourg, Mark, 46
Hannaford, J.F., (Lieut. Col.), 94
Harris, B.A. (Reverend), 48
Harris, Jim, 104
Harrison, R., 106
Harvey, John (Colonel), 20, 21
Hayes, James, 40
Heddle, Eva Marlene, 51, 52
Heddle, Malcolm, 52
Helka, Fred, 104
Henning Park, 106
Her Majesty, Queen Elizabeth II, 22
Hewitt Block, 91
Hewitt, Clarence, 91, 94
Hewitt, Mary Ann (Overend), 91, 94
Hewitt, Sydney, 91, 93, 94
Hewitt, Thomas, 91
Hicks, T.J., 101
Highway 6, 41, 42, 86, 88
Highway 54, 19, 25, 54, 78
Hill, Aaron, 19
Hillhouse Farm, 17, 18, 19, 20, 21
Hilmer, A. (Fire Chief), 48
Holmes, William, 86
House of Commons, 52, 53
Hudspeth, Bruce, 103
Hudspeth, Joseph, 34, 97
Hudspeth, Robert, 33
Huff Tract, 22

Indianna, 16, 24
Ingles, Jim, 89
Insolvent Act, 36
Iron Bridge, 75, 76
Iroquois Indian Museum, 66

Jackson, John, 16
Jenkins, Roland, 104
Jessie (tugboat), 23
John Builder Furniture Factory, 61
John Scott & Co., 38
Johnson, Emily (Howells), 54

Johnson, E. Pauline, 53, 54, 55, 56, 57
Johnson, George H.M. (Mohawk Chief), 54, 55
Johnson, John Smoke, 55
Johnston, Mr. & Mrs., 19
Jones, Albert E., 95, 96, 105, 106
Jones Bakery, 95, 96
Jones Catering, 97
Jones Debbie, 95, 97
Jones, Jean, 96, 97
Jones, Harold, 95, 96, 97
Jones, Hugh, 95, 97

Karighwaycagh (Catherine Munn), 18
Kelly, Dennis, 30
Kerr, Thomas Cockburn, 42
King Edward VII, 54
King George V, 59
King, MacKenzie (Prime Minister), 53
Kinnear, Helen, 101, 102
Kinsmen Park, 68, 106
Klink, Carl F., 18
Kohler Bros., 30

Lady Onondaga (river boat), 109
Lake Erie, 15, 96
Lake Huron, 26
Landers, Wally (Dr.), 103
Last Duel in Canada, 17, 20
Lauder, Harry, 49
Laurier, Wilfrid (Sir), 59
Lawson, Sandy, 99
Leousis, Chris, 40
Leousis, Louis, 40
Lickers, Al, 103
Lickers, Cliff, 103
Lincoln Township, 91
Lions Park, 106
Little, Ann, 41
Little, Charles, 41
Little, Harriet, 41
Little, James, 39, 40, 41, 42, 78
Little, James (Jr.), 42
Little, John, 41
Little, Leonard, 41
Little, Margaret Jane, 41, 42
Little's Post Office, 41
Little, William, 41, 42
Local Architectural Conservation Advi-

sory Committee (LACAC), 78
Locker, Alvin, 105
Longboat, Harvey, 104
Lower Grand River Trust, 24, 25
Lucerne Seed (No. 1), 42

MacDonald, Randolph, 74
MacGregor Concert Bureau, 29, 46, 47
MacGregor, Donald, 46
MacGregor, Jean, 46
MacGregor, Jesslie Cameron, 46, 47, 48, 49
Mackay, Eccleston, 56
Mackie, Eino, 106
Mackie, Helen, 90
Mahoney, T.J., 74
Mansion House, 41
Market Square, 67
Marshall Concession, 64
Marston, William, 42
Martin, Bob, 103
Martindale, Arrell (Arley), 82, 90
Martindale, Barbara, 82, 83
Martindale, Chester (Ches), 82, 103, 105
Martindale, Harrison, 64, 65, 82
McCallum, J.D., 48
McGregor & Co., 69
McKenzie, William Lyon, 36
McKinnon, Archibald, 37, 39
McKinnon, Catherine, 37
McKinnon, Christina, 37, 39
McKinnon, Donald, 37
McKinnon, Euphemia, 37, 39
McKinnon, Flora, 37, 39
McKinnon, Isabella, 37
McKinnon, John, 37, 39
McKinnon, Malcolm, 37
McKinnon, Mary, 37
McKinnon, Neil, 38
McKinnon, Ranald (Dr.), 38
McKinnon, Ranald (Squire), 13, 17, 23, 35, 36, 37, 38, 39, 42, 60
McKinnon, Sophia (Matthews), 39
McKinnon Woollen Mill, 27, 36, 50, 60
McKinnon Sawmill, 106
McLean, Terry, 103
McLean, Mr., 28
McMaster, Bob, 103
McMillan, Reverend, 52

McQuarrie (Daniel), Thorburn (James), Munro, William partnership, 49
McQuarrie, Laughlan, 39, 49
Meighen, Arthur (Rt. Hon.), 52, 53
Mellish, Bert, 41
Mellish, Mary, 41
Mendelssohn Choir, 59
Methodist Church, 40
Merrell, H.S., 60
Messenger, Thomas, 81, 82, 83
Middleport, 55
Miller, Bud, 103, 105
Milton, 57, 58, 87
Milton Historical Society, 58
Misener, Tom, 103
Moerschfelder, Bob, 103
Moffat, R., 106
Mohawk, 15, 17, 19, 22, 54, 55
Mohawk Chapel, 22
Mohawk (sailing ship), 24
Montreal, 87
Moore, Elizabeth, 42
Moore, William, 42
Moore, William Henry, 42
Moore, William Henry Marston, 42
Montreal, 42
Moraviantown, 21
Morrison, Bev, 90
Morrison, D., 106
Morrison, Tom, 106
Morrison, Tom (family), 87
Morrison, W., 106
Moyer, W., 106
Munn, Catherine (Maus, Mons, Docherty), 18, 19, 20
Munro, William, 41, 42, 49
Murphy, Belle, 41
Murphy, J., 68
Murphy, Jack, 41
Murray, Ken, 103
Murton, Fanny (Mrs. Alfred Walker), 58

Nanticoke, 31
National Hockey League, 105
"Neighbourly News", (CBC), 103
Neilson, K., 106
Nelles, Henry, 15, 16
Newfoundland Capital Corporation (N.C.C.), 83

New York World, 82
Niagara, 18, 19, 21
Niagara Gleaner, 21
Niagara River, 26
Nith River, 26
Northern Ireland, 41, 42
Norton, John (Captain) (Major), 17, 18, 19, 20, 21, 22
Norton, John (Jr.), 19, 20, 21, 22

Oakville, 48
Old Boys and Old Girls Reunion, 29, 77, 99, 100
Ohio River, 18
Ohsweken, 53, 54, 64
Oneida Village, 17, 33, 35
Oneida Township, 13, 15, 16
Onondaga, 102
Onondaga (sailing ship), 24, 102
Ontario Department of Public Highways, 73, 74
Ontario Heritage Foundation, 58
Ontario Hockey League, 103, 105
Ontario Ministry of Citizenship and Culture, 58, 66
Opera House, 43, 44, 45, 74
O'Rourke, Margaret, 60
Orpheus Male Choir, 47
Otter Publishing, 82, 83
Ouse River, 16
Overend, Sam, 68

Paisley Square, 67
Parke, Stan, 62
Paris, 28, 55, 79, 86
Paris Junction, 26
Parker, Jim, 103
Parker, Peter, 103
Patterson, Mrs., 33
Peart, Alf, 79
Pedlow, Henry, 39
Peirson, Dave, 103
Peirson, Reg, 103
Perth County, 52
Peterborough, 105
Phillips, Jim, 90
Phillips, Thomas, 17
Picton, 105
Pomeroy, Brick, 81

Port Colborne, 83
Port Dover, 28, 35, 36, 41, 59, 96, 102
Port Dover (freight boat), 24
Port Maitland, 26
Porter, Victor, 104
Pottruff, N., 106
Pressman's Printing, 83

Queen Anne, 22
Queen, The (steamship), 24
Queen Victoria, 33

Randolph Macdonald Co. Ltd., 74
Red Jacket (steamship), 24, 26
Regional Municipality of Halidmand
  Norfork, 71
Regional News This Week, 83
Rice, Margaret Jane (Little), 42
Rice, Edmond Spring (Hon.), 42
Richards, Danny, 103
Richardson (family), 40
Richardson Apartments, 63
Richardson, Matthew, 41
Rideau Canal, 16, 35
Robertson, Annie, 57
Robertson, Hutton, 57
Robertson, Isa, 57
Robertson, Jessie, 57
Robertston, John, 57
Robertson, John (Jr.), 57
Robertson, Peter Lymburner, 57, 58
Robertson (P.L.P Manufacturing Com-
  pany), 57, 58
Robertson, Will, 57
Robertson Whitehouse Company, 58
Robertston Screw (nail), 57, 58
Robinson Blackmore Group, 83
Roper Block, 43
Roper Drug Store, 44
Round Table Quarterly, 59
Royal Canadian Institute, 59
Royal Ontario Museum, 59
Runchey, Melvin, 77
Rushton, Ruth, 49
Ruthven, 24, 25
Ruthven Management Committee, 24
Ruthven Park, 24, 25
Ryan, "Bolt", 41
Ryan Hotel, 41

Ryan, John, 41

Sabo, E., 106
Sabo, F., 106
Sachem, 81
Sawle, Henry B., 65, 67, 82
Sawle, Mary Florence, 82, 99
Sawle, W.T., 82
Schull, Joseph, 59
Scotland, 17, 19, 35, 42, 87, 88
Scott, Douglas, 50
Scott, Hugh, 50
Scott's Iron Foundry, 27, 61, 75, 84, 85
Scott, John, 84
Scott, Osborne Thomas (O.T.) (Ob), 14,
  49, 50, 51, 99, 100, 110
Scott, William, 49, 50
Seldon's Bakery Shop, 95, 96
Seneca and Oneida Agricultural Society,
  33
Seneca Bridge, 77, 78, 107
Seneca Hill, 40
Seneca House, 59
Seneca Park, 77
Seneca Village, 16, 17, 33, 35, 39, 40, 41,
  59, 62, 84
Seneca Township, 13, 15, 57, 58, 91
Serblan, Brune, 103
Shea, H. 106
Shipman, Brent, 103
Shippey, George, 110
Shirra, Robert, 33, 50
Shoots and Avery Carriage Shop, 27
Simcoe, 28, 69
Simpson, F. (Variety Store), 44
Sims Lock, 16, 19
Six Nations Confederacy, 15, 18,19, 24,
  54
Six Nations Reserve, 13, 54, 64, 65, 109
Small, Eric, 90
Small, Keith, 90
Smith, R., 106
Smith, Ron, 104
Smith, T., 68
Spratt, Roy, 106
Spratt, Tommy, 105
South Seneca, 16, 35
Speed River, 26
Squamish Reserve, 56

St. Andrew's Lodge, 44
St. Andrew's Square, 67
Stanley Park (B.C.), 54
Steward, Hugh (Captain), 38
St. Paul's Anglican Church, 45, 61
St. Patrick's Catholic Church, 48
St. Thomas, 21, 69
Stelco (Steel Company), 88
Stotts, Ann, 46
Stotts, Bill (Constable), 45, 46
Strachan, John (Dr.), 19
Streetsville, 36
Sullivan, Mrs. Patrick (Eva Marlene Heddle), 52
Sunnyside, 17, 35
Sutherland (family), 40
Swallow (tugboat), 23
Szabo, Frank, 62

Talman, James J., 18
Tekahionwake (Pauline Johnson), 57
Teyoninkokarawen (Captain John Norton), 17
Thames River, 21
Thamesville, 22
Thayendanegea (Joseph Brant), 15
Thompson, Andrew, 25
Thompson, Andrew (Colonel), 25
Thompson, Bob, 30, 42
Thompson, David, 25
Thompson, David, 24, 25
Thompson, David (M.P.) 24, 25, 36
Thompson, Fred, 79
Thompson, Helen, 42
Thompson, R.J., 74
Thompson, Robert, 19, 22
Thomson, S., 106
Tillsonburg, 83
Toll House, 75, 79, 80
Toll Keeper, 80
Toronto, 36, 53, 56, 59
Toronto Art Gallery, 59
Toronto Conservatory of Music, 46, 59
Toronto Star, 51
Toronto Symphony Orchestra, 46
Town Hall, 33, 45, 49, 67, 69, 70, 71, 72, 85, 97, 100
Town of Haldimand, 73, 78
Tregaskis, H., 68

Trotter, Elizabeth (Mrs.), 53
Tuffy (Lloyd A. Culp), 63, 64
Turner, Jacob, 16, 23, 35
Turner, John, 69
Tuscarora (sailing ship), 24
Tutton, James, 80
Tweedsmuir History, 97
Tweedsmuir, Lady, 97

Union Hotel, 28, 29, 74
United Empire Loyalists (Loyalists), 15
University of Toronto, 52
Upper Canada, 18, 38

Vancouver, 53, 56, 57

Walker, Alfred E., 58, 59
Walker, Barbara Lang, 73
Walker, Byron Edmund (Sir), 58, 59
Walker, Fanny (Burton)
Walker, R.E., 60
War of 1812-14, 18, 20
War-Time Elections Act, 52
Welland Canal, 16
Welsman, Frank, 46
Westinghouse, 88
Westroc, 88
Whitelaw, Lawrence "Whitey", 104
Williamson (farm), 42
Winegard, William, 101, 102
Winegard, John, 103
Winger, Earl, 106
Wingham, 83
Winnipeg, 52
Wolkowski, Stan, 103
Woodland Cultural Education Centre, 66
World War I, 91, 97
World War II, 88, 96, 97

York, 15, 16, 24, 25, 27, 86, 95
York-Grand River Historical Society, 78
Young, Adam, 15, 16
Young, Chris, 59
Young, Phil, 68
Young, Tom, 103
Yukon, 57

Barbara A. Martindale is the publisher of the *Grand River Sachem*. Her popular column "For What It's Worth" appears weekly. Prominently identified with many community organizations, the author is also an active member of the Media Club of Canada, Hamilton Branch. The former Member Services Director of the Canadian Community Newspapers Association is well-known nationally within Canada's print media.